A SALUTE TO ANN ALDRICH

If you were a lesbian in the 1950s, you were probably married, with children. Or solitary, drudging in the hinterlands. . . . Could you be the only woman on the planet with tender feelings for other women? Were you evil? Cursed? Or merely sick? . . . And then a miracle happened. In the drug store, the train station, the bus stop, the newsstand, you came across a rack of pulp paperbacks. Among the cow̲ -and-robbers, and the science ꞈ ̲ ̲ut lesbians. Sud- denly, you ̲ ̲ ̲ ̲ community of unknown si ̲ ̲

Some o ̲ ̲ ̲ ̲ ̲ ̲cretly, were fic- tional roman ̲ ̲ ̲ ̲ ̲ ̲ heartaches, they provided solace and ero ̲ ̲ ̲ ̲ ̲ansport. But another genre appeared: factual reports about lesbian life in the big city, penned by someone who lived there and knew. Her name was Ann Aldrich, and two of her best-known books—*We Walk Alone* and *We, Too, Must Love*—are now being reissued.

Aldrich told you what it was like to come out (joyful prospect!). She told you where lesbians in the know gathered— the bars, the resorts, the restaurants. She told you what these women wore, how they talked, how they coped with intricate personal problems. You were amazed to discover that there were different lifestyles within the nascent lesbian community: high and low, butch and femme, uptown and low-down.

There were even men in the lives of many of them. How did that work? It was a veritable Michelin Guide. You were riveted to the page. . . .

The effect on women was electric. From every corner of cre- ation, they wrote wrenching letters of relief and gratitude. Some were saved from suicide, the only solution to their dilemma they could conceive. Aldrich herself was taken aback at the outpour- ing of emotion.

—Ann Bannon,
author of *Odd Girl Out* and *The Beebo Brinker Chronicles*
July 2006

WE
WALK
ALONE

Other Works by Ann Aldrich:
We, Too, Must Love (1958)
Carol in a Thousand Cities (1960)
We Two Won't Last (1963)
Take a Lesbian to Lunch (1972)

WE
WALK
ALONE

ANN ALDRICH

Introduction by Marijane Meaker
Afterword by Stephanie Foote

The Feminist Press
at the City University of New York
New York

Published by the Feminist Press at the City University of New York
The Graduate Center
365 Fifth Avenue
New York, NY 10016
www.feministpress.org

First Feminist Press Edition, 2006.

Originally published by Fawcett Publications in 1955.

Library of Congress Cataloging-in-Publication Data

Aldrich, Ann, 1927 May 27-
  We walk alone / Ann Aldrich ; introduction by Marijane Meaker ;
afterword by Stephanie Foote. -- 1st Feminist press ed.
    p. cm.
  Prev. ed. entered under Marijane Meaker.
  ISBN-13: 978-1-55861-525-0 (pbk.)
  ISBN-10: 1-55861-525-3 (pbk.)
  ISBN-13: 978-1-55861-526-7 (library)
  ISBN-10: 1-55861-526-1 (library)
  1. Lesbians. 2. Lesbianism. I. Meaker, Marijane, 1927- We walk
alone. II. Title.
  HQ75.5.A28 2006
  306.76'630973--dc22
                                2006021212

This publication was made possible, in part, through the support of
Diane Bernard in honor of Joan R. Heller, Don Linn, and Dorothy Sander and
Joyce Warshow.

Text design by Lisa Force
Printed in Canada by Transcontinental Printing

10 09 08 07 06   5 4 3 2 1

CONTENTS

INTRODUCTION TO THE 2006 EDITION

Under the pseudonym Donald Webster Cory in 1951 Edward Sagarin wrote a groundbreaking examination of male homosexuality. He had originally thought of using the name Don Cory, a reverse of *Corydon*, the name of Andre Gide's book written for young gay men. But Sagarin's publisher thought the name too unusual, feared litigation, and convinced Sagarin to be Donald instead of Don and to add Webster as a middle name.

The Homosexual in America was an immediate success.

I was both impressed and inspired by the book. It was really a guide to the life—the history, the laws, the books, the bars—everything an emerging gay man needed to know.

It was not pertinent to lesbians. Male and female lives have always been so very different that political activists eventually insisted on not grouping us all under one banner. The correct usage became "lesbians and gay men," instead of simple "homosexuals."

After I read Cory's masterpiece, I became determined to write a book like it, for lesbians. I had already flabbergasted Fawcett Publications, Gold Medal Books, when my little story of lesbianism in a college sorority outsold the paperback edition of *God's Little Acre*, by Erskine Caldwell. The publishers had had no such expectations for that paperback, selling for 25 cents. My editor had even changed the name *Sorority Girl* to *Spring Fire* (1952), hoping to confuse the audience for James A. Michener's best-selling *Fires of Spring*, and perhaps pick up more sales.

This same editor, Dick Carroll, a sharp fellow from Hollywood, new to paperback publishing, was enthusiastic about the idea of writing a female version of Cory's book. I had chosen the pseudonym Vin Packer for the Gold Medal Books, and to my surprise one of them had received a great Sunday *New York Times* review by crime critic Anthony Boucher. This was not a book about lesbians, but a suspense book, a fictional murder mystery.

I decided to continue to write books that could be reviewed, even in paperback. The crime field was best for this, and so I decided Vin Packer would remain a mystery/suspense writer.

Pseudonyms were common in those days for writers with a homosexual agenda. Some critics felt Gore Vidal had ruined his literary reputation when he wrote *The City and the Pillar* under his own name. It did not get a *New York Times* review, or any review in the usual media.

For my first venture into nonfiction journalism with lesbianism my subject matter, I though of the name Bianca Blye.

Dick Carroll said, "No, no, NO! Do you want to be confused with Captain Bligh? We need a soft, all-American name, like that young man in the radio serial, Henry Aldrich."

"Ann Aldrich," I suggested.

"That's perfect!" said Dick.

I chose the title *We Walk Alone*. I wanted to suggest isolation and our stalwart nature. I wanted a simple, clear title. I never wanted the subtitle Gold Medal put on the cover, "Through Lesbos Lonely Groves." But in those days, young writers had little to say about subtitles, cover copy, or cover art.

Such concerns seemed not to matter to the buyers of *We Walk Alone*. The important selling point was simply that this was a book about lesbians: true stories and facts. In the fifties it was impossible to find anything on the subject that wasn't intentionally pornographic. Certain straight men have always had a prurient interest in us.

Although there was no mention of Vin Packer on the cover, a little sales boost I wouldn't allow because I wanted to keep Packer identified with suspense, Ms. Aldrich did not need Ms. Packer. She did just fine for herself, selling millions of copies. Ms. Aldrich also got more mail from readers than any author at Fawcett Publications had ever received. Boxes of it were waiting for me whenever I went to see Dick to talk about the next book.

The letters to Ann Aldrich were mainly from young women. Some just wanted to tell their stories, and some wanted to come to New York. Where should they live? What kind of jobs were there? Where were lesbian bars? How could they meet lesbians besides going to bars?

I answered most of these letters, telling the writers honestly that I had no information about apartments or employment, and that the bars opened and closed from time to time, and so they would have to discover the new places for themselves. I also told them about an organization for lesbians called The Daughters of Bilitis and a lesbian magazine they might subscribe to called *The Ladder*. I had had my quarrels with that magazine because of their hostile portrayals of heterosexual men, and because I thought their fiction was gross, but it was the only one. Take it or leave it.

Mail that came from males was sparse and most often included boasts of sex prowess, the "all you need is a good man" response. A few females enclosed very explicit naked poses of themselves.

But mostly, this book received the attention of an audience long ignored, either through ignorance of its existence or on moral grounds.

We Walk Alone enjoyed several printings.

Although there were a few organizations for male homosexual activists both in Manhattan and San Francisco, and the very small Daughters of Bilitis organization which published *The Ladder*, I wanted to write about the average New York City lesbian. In the fifties, we felt no entitlement, and most of us were wary of any organizations. The fifties was famous for its witch-hunts and congressional investigations. In the eyes of the law we were illegal, and religions viewed us as anathema. I wanted to write about what it was like to live in one of the most sophisticated cities in the world, and find yourself unacceptable because of your sexual orientation. I was not interested then in politics or causes, nor by nature was I a revolutionary. I thought of myself as a reporter, describing the good and bad of our world.

I hoped, too, that Ann Aldrich wouldn't lack a sense of humor. We may have walked alone, but many of us had come to the big city—the Apple—to find someone who would end the loneliness. We were looking, too, for a place where we could thrive and excel. This courageous journey brought with it many tears, and much laughter: ironies and epiphanies. I wanted Ann Aldrich to record them. *We Walk Alone* began as the first book in what would become the Aldrich series.

Marijane Meaker
East Hampton
2006

FOREWORD

This book is the result of fifteen years of participation in society as a female homosexual. It is written with the conviction that there is a sincere need and demand for further enlightenment on this subject. I am convinced that the opinions and viewpoints of the lesbian herself are as valuable in arriving at conclusions about her nature as are those proffered by the psychiatrist, sociologist, anthropologist, jurist, churchman, or psychologist.

The information the professional imparts is that of the objective "outsider." His hypotheses are reached by a studious surveillance of the homosexual element that presents itself to him in his work. Whether it be in the form of a maladjusted patient under analysis, a peculiar "trend" discerned in recent mass media, an interesting folkway observed in Balinese culture, a sodomist run afoul of the law, a distraught layman seeking spiritual counsel, or a revealing reaction on a Rorschach test, the skilled professional can never hope to apply his hypotheses to a cross section of homosexuals. He works within the limits of his experiences and those of his colleagues.

The information I shall offer in this book is that of the subjective "insider," and it is intended as a supplement to those assumptions already recorded by conscientious professional people. I hope not only to disclose facets of the broader and more typical female homosexual life, but to give voice to much of the opinion from within this group.

The material I shall employ has been gleaned from original study, free discussion with professional people who have investigated various aspects of homosexuality in the female, frequent conversations with actual lesbians, and personal experience.

The scope of my work is meant to include not only overt, practicing lesbian experience—though this will take up a large part of the book—but also the experiences of the homosexual who finds outlets other than the physical for her homosexual inclinations, and the more seriously ill repressed homosexual who fights an enemy she can neither see nor call by name, but which she carries within her like a cancer.

It is my wish that *We Walk Alone* may bring more compassionate understanding on the part of mothers and fathers, sisters and brothers, friends, teachers, employers, and strangers, who may at some time in their lives be confronted with homosexuality in their midst. I hope too that my book will contribute something toward encouraging a greater tolerance of this minority, and that it will hearten those homosexuals, like myself, who are earnestly trying to resolve the perplexing problems that face them in their daily living.

I am particularly grateful to Dr. Gurbax Waraich for the insight he lent me into this problem during our many discussions of this material, and for all the valuable help I have received from Dr. Florence Shea in our conversations concerning this project.

Ann Aldrich
New York
1955

1.   WHO IS SHE?

"I can always tell a 'lessie,'" a young Yale man who claimed to be a student of psychology told me one Saturday evening as he sat beside me in a Greenwich Village "gay" bar, frequented by many female homosexuals. "And I don't mean just the kind you see in here. These are obvious types. I mean the discreet 'lessies,' the ones who try to cover up, the ones who wouldn't be caught dead in a joint like this. I can spot them every time. Even the real subtle ones. Eventually they give themselves away."

I asked him to elaborate, and he said, "There are various telltale signs. Some you know by their choice in clothes. They wear suits a lot, and tailored blouses. They jump at the chance to buy any new boyish-styled fashions that these fairy designers dream up for them. Like the button-down shirts Brooks Brothers started carrying a few years back for women, and the trench coats with the belt in the back, copying the man's style, and the kilts with the high socks, and the vests, and the slacks and shorts with the fly front—all made for women. Some gals refused to be defeminized; others went along on a couple of items; and a few went whole hog like kids in a department-store toyland at Christmastime. They're the same few that hustled out and had their hair cut off when the Italian-boy cuts came along, and shelled out for women's pipes at the first

rumor of a cancer scare for cigarette smokers. Do you understand what I'm getting at? Just give these 'lessies' an inch of
encouragement to be more masculine, and they'll walk the
mile."

"You seem to know an awful lot about lesbians," I said.

"I've made a study of them," he told me proudly. "Once
you know the clues, you never have any trouble picking them
out."

As we talked further, the young man enlightened me as to
other "clues." Lesbians favor little finger-rings. Lesbians like
cigarette holders. (This, he explained rather condescendingly,
if not too clearly, had something to do with penis envy.) Lesbians are good at sports; indeed, he informed me that most
gym teachers are "lessies," as are a majority of women athletes.
Lesbians drink more than most women, and they drink their
liquor "neat" or "on the rocks." Lesbians want careers; they
like to "show men up" in the business world. Lesbians are
more intellectual than average females; they read more, know
more about art and music and scoff at men who aren't interested in these things. Lesbians who date men try to tear them
down, instead of building them up; they are cold; their kisses
are proffered as great favors. Lesbians argue a lot. Lesbians are
more interested in politics than other women are. Lesbians
curse. Lesbians talk out of the sides of their mouths. Lesbians
like to tell dirty jokes in mixed company, and act like "one of
the boys." Lesbians like big dogs like boxers and police dogs to
protect them from the man they always imagine is out to
attack them.

"Lesbians," the young man concluded, "have one or two,
many, or all of these traits. I know one when I see her!"

If the boy from Yale had been correct in his assumptions
about the ingredients that go into a lesbian's makeup, he
would have the edge on every student of psychology, psychiatry, and sociology, from Freud to Henry to Kinsey. The fact of

the matter is that lesbianism cannot be accurately defined, nor can the lesbian's personality traits be lumped into any category that will include all of her characteristics, and yet exclude those of the remainder of the female population.

Who is the lesbian?

She is many women.

Look at her, and she cannot be distinguished from her more normal sisters. Test her mental development, and she ranges from feeble-minded to superior. Examine her background, and she comes from the smoky slums of Pittsburgh; the exclusive homes of Oak Park, Illinois; the sprawling campuses of Cornell, Radcliffe, Michigan, Stephens; the boxed-in Lower East Side of New York City; the sun-baked open plains of Texas and Wyoming. Expose her to psychotherapy, and she is "undersexed" and "oversexed," man-hungry and a man-hater; an overt participant with a "girl friend," a repressed homosexual with a husband and a family; a secretary with a crush on her female boss, a divorcee with nymphomaniac tendencies, a society matron, a widower, a teen-aged high-school girl, a whore.

There is no stereotype in the over-all picture of the lesbian. This is the first discovery I ever made about the group of which I am a member.

I have seen the professional "butches" in all the Greenwich Villages from Los Angeles to Paris. These girls make careers of their abnormality, displaying themselves in homosexual hangouts for whatever pittance they are able to maneuver—a sandwich on the house, bought by the management, who exploits them; a whisky bought by a lonely sailor; a five-dollar bill from a curious party of tourists who want them to sit down and tell how they got "that way"; a pickup by some prostitute who spends her wages supporting less industrious lesbians; and often as not at the end of the evening a "roll job" in an alley, performed deftly by one who has had her eye all evening on the fellow with the thick wallet sitting at the bar, and getting drunker with each round he orders.

I have seen the innocent crushes between young girls, prevalent in most boarding schools, where the sight of boys their own age is a rarity, grow from tender concern to violent passion. Hands that at first merely passed notes in study hall became hands that caressed one another in lovers' fashion after "lights out" in a darkened room along a lonely dormitory corridor.

I have seen the more sophisticated big-city "gay" women, whose lavish parties are attended exclusively by homosexuals, many times with males included. There I have met actresses, advertising people, publishing people, musicians, society women, husbands and wives who have married one another to ward off any suspicions on the part of their normal friends and their families; dancers, designers, buyers, writers, and realtors. In some of these self-assured cliques, homosexuality is as fashionable as heterosexuality is unfathomable.

I have seen the lesbians who live ostensibly as roommates, whether in a sorority house on a Midwestern campus, a rooming house in Salisbury, North Carolina, or an apartment house in New York City. They date men; often they double-date. Sometimes their dates are a defense against gossip; sometimes they are offered as proof to themselves that they are not truly pure homosexuals, but bisexuals.

I have seen the extremely feminine lesbians who choose only very masculine partners; in many instances actual transvestites whose male appearances fool even the wary observer. Because these "fems" must support their butches, who either cannot find work because of their masquerade or more often dislike work even when it is available to them, they invariably become "hookers," or whores, while the more energetic butch sometimes pimps for her girl. If whoring does not pay amply, dope peddling might, and more than one of this sort of prostitute has found herself an addict.

In gay bars of vast assortment, from the frowzy to the plush, I have seen the wholesome-looking, twentyish blonde, swathed in a creamy polo coat, buying drinks for a sullen-faced, boyish brunette her same age, saying, "But don't you understand? If my mother and father ever found out about us, they'd kill me! And you too, darling! That's why you mustn't call me at home—ever!"; the pretty, liquid-eyed sixteen-year-old who wanders in with a couple of her school chums, "just to see what it's like," self-consciously accepting a suave Negro butch's invitation to "Dance, honey?"; the haggard, middle-aged teletype operator in the pin-striped woman's suit, nursing a beer and listening to the lyrics of "Lush Life," telling anyone who will listen about the beautiful girl she used to have; the poor people's Tallulah Bankhead, in dark glasses, strutting back and forth in a shaggy fox jacket, a satin dress, and spike heels, her hair lustrous and loose at her shoulders, laughing raucously at her own jokes while she waits for "my girl" to arrive, and murmurs frequently, "Now, damn! Where *is* that chick? She should have been here by now!"; the graceful elder woman with the impeccable English accent, her arm wrapped around a fawning peroxide blonde still in her "show clothes" from an uptown club where she performs; the studious college seniors who claim to be there only in the interests of research, their hands touching gently under the table; the pair of smart-looking, urbane women executives at a table in a corner getting high on Rob Roys; the ugly, deformed creature in the man's overalls, with a huge bosom, frizzy hair, a scarred face, and a soft, lonely voice, finding some peculiar solace in a world where men don't matter; the good, the frightened, the beautiful, the bad, the ignorant, the confident, the uncertain, the intelligent, and the mean—they are everywhere homosexuals gather, and they are incognito in the dominant society of the normal.

I have seen them often, know them, watched them, listened

to them, talked with them, lived with them, and been a part of their life. I have seen them, and I am one of them; yet I have never been able to pick a lesbian out of a crowd. There is no definition, no formula, no pattern that will accurately characterize the female homosexual.

She is any woman.

Are there many of us?

The section of the Kinsey report pertaining to male homosexuality dropped like a bombshell on the unsuspecting public. Braced for a similar explosion in the subsequent study of the American female, Kinsey readers were confronted with little more than a mild firecracker. With the figure set below 4 per cent, a much smaller percentage than the 10 per cent of the male population that had been estimated as being homosexuals, Kinsey researchers disproved any notion that there is a vast number of female homosexuals. The validity of his findings, as well as the estimates of men like Havelock Ellis, George W. Henry, Ford and Beach, and other old and new astute researchers, can be questioned, argued, and discussed interminably, without conclusion. The glaring fact remains that there is probably no way of calculating the true proportion of homosexuals, male or female.

Whether or not male homosexuality is more frequent than female homosexuality, certainly outward evidences of the former are displayed much more often than those of lesbianism. There are two possible explanations for this. One is that the lesbian camouflages her abnormality more easily than her male counterpart is able to do. Women, in sharp contrast to men, go arm and arm along the streets, address one another as "darling" and "honey," embrace quite openly, often share the same bed as roommates, and generally indulge in open gestures of affection without arousing any suspicions in the community.

The tomboy stage in a young girl's life is accepted as a normal phase of her development, whereas any proclivity toward the "sissy" in the young boy is promptly counteracted with box-ing lessons and Boy Scouts. In the eyes of the mother of a teen-aged daughter, blue jeans and flannel shirts are just part of the high-school girls' fads; a parallel feminine inclination in the son of the family is a worrisome symptom of a morbid disorder.

A woman today is free to enter almost any profession she chooses, from engineering to medicine to the Marine Corps, with little speculation from others as to her normality or fem-ininity. The war years resulted in the final emancipation of women. But male designers, decorators, hairdressers, ballet dancers, artists, and nurses continually find their lines of work maligned by innuendos.

The female homosexual who cares to be discreet knows little restriction in her personality, appearance, or choice of profession. Her presence in a business establishment, in a restaurant, along the boulevard, or at a party is inconspicuous. If her hair is cut ear-length, it is a new style. If she walks with giant strides, and stands with legs spread and arms akimbo, she is forceful, aggressive, and probably a good golfer. She can wear slacks and shirts virtually anywhere. If her voice is pitched differently than most women's, she is the sultry type.

Not so the male. In the recent Broadway play *Tea and Sympathy*, by Robert Anderson, the young hero, forlorn at his colleagues' accusations that he is "queer," implores his room-mate, a husky, virile football player, to teach him how to walk. A favorite criticism of the male homosexual is "the way he walks."

"The fag," a disgusted man said to me at a party one evening, as he noted the entrance of a lithe fellow with minc-ing steps, "like the fog, comes on little cat feet!"

A man, if he is to be respected as a man, must walk like a man, speak up like a man, with a man's good deep voice, stand like a man, dress like a man, and fight, eat, love, drink, and die like a man.

The emasculated male is a misfit in the world of men; an insult to them; a stain on their clean blotter of ripping masculinity; a curious creature who causes discomfort and stimulates anger, and a spectacle akin to a freak.

A second explanation for the seemingly greater number of male homosexuals than of female homosexuals can be found in their propensity for promiscuity, and for gatherings of their clan. There are countless bars and cafés all over the world that cater exclusively to the male homosexual trade. Their promiscuity has made them infamous in the eyes of society. In the public parks of cities like New York, Washington, Baltimore, and Chicago, a silent sunset gun seems to set off the hunt of one male homosexual for another. In bars, steam baths, subway stations, and washrooms, the normal male is many times solicited by his abnormal brother.

While it is not unusual for an ordinary man to find himself on the receiving end of one of these homosexuals' preliminary advances, it is rare indeed for the average woman to be approached by a lesbian. The female homosexual, for reasons I shall discuss in later chapters, shies from any such behavior, as a rule, just as she does from open meetings with her own kind. In proportion to the number of male homosexual bars and cafés, lesbian hangouts are relatively scarce. Even there, the lesbian is less prone to "pressure" a likely subject than is the male in a similar situation.

Because the female homosexual masks her abnormality with chameleon-like dexterity, because she is less disposed to promiscuous and indiscriminate relations, and because, as Freud once wrote, she "has not only been ignored by the law, but has also been neglected by psychoanalytic research," the ostensible scarcity of her species makes her a more interesting, if not a more sympathetic, character than the male homosexual.

"He's a fairy!" whispered in a public place, does not usually inspire half as much concern as "She's a lesbian!" People may turn once to view the fairy; they turn twice and a third time to see the lesbian.

"It's an odd thing," a New York City publisher told me once, "but novels about male homosexuals just don't sell the way those dealing with female homosexuals do. Either the public is more curious about lesbian life, or it's repulsed by the fairy's. It doesn't seem so bad, somehow, to read about two women kissing one another—but men? Uh-uh!"

Perhaps the best proof of this remark is in the fact that probably the most well-known novel about homosexuality in the English language is Radclyffe Hall's *The Well of Loneliness*, a story of lesbianism. No book written about male homosexuality enjoys such notoriety. Capitalizing on the general public's familiarity with that title, movie houses billed Colette's sensitive story of homosexuality in a French boarding school for girls, *Olivia*, as *The Pit of Loneliness*. Although this motion picture was made in France, where such subject matter seems to be handled far less vitriolically, the fact that American film people chose it as one of the few French films for import shows the ever widening curiosity of the public about lesbianism.

In the past decade, sophisticated society has adopted an inquiring disposition toward the prodigy of homosexuality in general. It is no longer considered intelligent to react with belligerence, distaste, or complete ignorance toward the abnormality. Today, a male or female who vigorously protests homosexuality as being ugly, lewd, or repulsive often meets with the retort "Methinks you do protest too much." As one psychiatrist with whom I discussed this put it, "It used to be that folks were afraid to show any interest in the subject for fear others would accuse them of being homosexual. Now, for the very same reason, they are afraid not to show an interest."

Thus, in this climate of concern, novels, plays, movies, psychological studies, short stories, and poems are more and more reflecting the various aspects of the homosexual's situation in relation to the more fortunate normal society. Despite the fact that the public seems to show a greater sympathy with the female homosexual than with the male, the mirror of mass media is held up less often to the lesbian's life.

The lesbian need not remain an enigma. In the following chapters an attempt will be made to unravel much of the mystery surrounding her.

2. HOW DID SHE GET THAT WAY?

Topsy, the little slave girl in *Uncle Tom's Cabin*, gave as an explanation for her existence the now immortal words "I 'spects I growed." The lesbian's answer to the same question might well be "I suspect I didn't grow."

As Helene Deutsch pointed out in her study of female sexuality, homosexual women very often go on playing at "mother and child," to the exclusion of the father, or the male. Some assume the active role of the mother, choosing young girls for their love objects; others play the passive role of the child they once were, selecting older, maternal women for protective lovers. In all, the clitoris is the primary organ of their sexual pleasure, just as it was when they were children.

Little girls, even before they are old enough to be aware that they are little girls, are aware of the small organ at the upper part of their vulva, known as the clitoris. Masturbation is the baby's first initiation into the world of eroticism, and she has accomplished it singlehanded. Then as her world enlarges she becomes aware immediately of her mother, eventually of her father. According to Freud, the normal female's maturity has a dual development, physiological and psychological. When she abandons the clitoris as the executive organ of sexual satisfaction in favor of the vagina, she also transfers to the father the love she felt for the mother. The woman who cannot so develop is likely to remain at the retarded homosexual level. Her love stays fixed on her mother, for whom she is ever seeking substitutes.

Adler insisted that this retardation is a voluntary one on the part of the homosexual female, who is unable to accept the fact that she does not have the penis she envies and willfully attempts to be like that male whose domination she refuses.

Whether it is an infantile fixation or a protest of masculinity, lesbianism is regarded as an arrest of development. Many women who are not homosexuals, however, have found their development arrested at the clitoral stage. While they cannot be considered sexually mature women, their immaturity did not take a homosexual turn. How does the female homosexual differ from those females?

What really makes a woman a lesbian?

"From age ten," a female who became a homosexual after an unsuccessful marriage told me, "up until the time I was ready to marry, my mother had hammered in the idea that sex was a dirty thing. Then suddenly a minister said words over my head, I had a husband, and I was supposed to believe that by some sort of magic sex was now beautiful and sacred. Well, I couldn't believe it. I couldn't unlearn the old lesson."

A basic fear of sexual relations, and of the man who might cause intercourse to occur, is a common factor contributing to the causes of homosexuality in girls. This fear, if planted early enough and cultivated consistently during early childhood and girlhood, can often resist the most intense rational efforts at weeding it out in later years.

Sometimes, even before the young girl is conscious of sexual feelings, distinct or indistinct, toward boys, overanxious parents warp her outlook and thwart her normal development with their zealous warnings and remonstrations about "the things boys can do to you."

"What are little boys made of?" the nursery rhyme asks,

and provides the answer: "Snips and snails and puppy dogs' tails. That's what little boys are made of!"

And little girls? "Sugar and spice and all things nice."

By the same token, as the little girl grows into her teens and becomes more and more aware of this other sex with whom she shares experiences in daily living on the playground, in school, and under the same roof, she is not infrequently admonished about the nasty make-up of little boys.

"Don't talk to any strange men!" is a favorite warning of parents to their young daughters. "Don't accept rides with strange men!" While it is certainly good advice, the stress is too often put upon men, instead of upon strangers in general.

A transvestite who has dressed "in drag" for years told me she had always felt protected by male clothing. "My dad ran off when I was born," she explained, "and all Mom could say about men was that they could ruin you. I used to think I was safe because I wore the same clothes they did, and didn't look like a woman."

"I don't want my daughter going on any dates with a boy in a car!" the father of a teen-aged friend of mine used to declare emphatically. "All he wants to do is get her on some back road and maul her! If I ever hear about it, she'll catch it good!"

Growing up in the era of Ford and his flivver, this father may well have had all too vivid memories of his own behavior on a date with someone else's daughter thirty years ago, when the automobile was synonymous with parking, petting, and promiscuity. Many times young people are punished for the sins they *might* commit, which are the same sins their parents *did* commit when they were young. Parents of sons worry over the possibilities of their boys' smoking, drinking, driving too fast, gambling, or "getting in with a bad crowd" in which such activities might be encouraged. If they worry about any sexual experiences their son might engage in, their greater concern is

14 WE WALK ALONEWE WALK ALONE

with his taking precautions so that he won't (a) get a disease, or (b) get a girl pregnant and have to marry her.

Parents of daughters, on the other hand, concentrate primarily on the problem of possible sexual liaisons, and many times their neurotic anxiety instills a morbid sense of guilt, shame, and horror in the young girl's attitude.

Dr. George W. Henry, in his recent study *Sex Variants* [1941], describes an example of this while relating the case history of a female homosexual. As a child, the girl had no idea where babies came from, until a little girl around the corner told her they came from the stomach, and the doctor cut pregnant women from the chin to below the navel. Menstruation was a shock to her, and any mention of it in front of her mother caused her mother to blush and stammer without offering any explanation for its occurrence. Even at the age of seventeen, the patient, while she associated habitually with boys, was thoroughly unconscious of sex. Her father, however, was not convinced of her innocence, and although her menstrual periods were often irregular, one time when she missed one he accused her of having been out behind the barn. His fixation was so great that he finally took her to a doctor to see if she were still a virgin. "After that," the girl recounted, "I couldn't hold my head up."

"A boy," my father used to caution me, "can go home afterward, take a shower, and be just like new. A girl is irrevocably marred!"

Statements like that, offered freely and frequently by nervous parents, are sufficient nourishment for a thriving fear of sex, and thus of the male animal, with whom sex is immediately identified.

"If you don't get yourself pregnant," I recently heard an irate mother shout at her teen-aged daughter, whom she suspected of petting with her new boy friend, "you'll get yourself talked about so no boy will want you! You'll be trash! Nice girls wait until they're married. No one asks the other kind. No one wants secondhand goods!"

This exhortation contains two strong seeds of fear found in full bloom in the mind of the woman who cannot find love with a man. Fear of pregnancy, with all its consequences, and the dread of sexual subordination to a man who might reject her after her surrender make the male of the species a rather frightening spectacle in the eyes of the young girl. Under such conditions, fondness for the same sex, which seems safer, may become overdeveloped, while the feeling for the opposite sex remains in its undeveloped form. If the girl victimized by these fears and a subsequent overdeveloped affection for her own sex encounters a female of similar tendencies, she may find a ready response to her outpouring of love. Together the pair may soon discover a way of satisfying their mutual passion, and of obtaining voluptuous sensations "without having anything to do with a man!"

Fear has many faces.

"It isn't that I'm afraid of men!" a lesbian protested to me once. "I just know women better!"

A lack of familiarity with the opposite sex can transform itself into fear very rapidly. Because sexual intercourse is attended by many more taboos and far more disagreeable consequences in the case of the young girl than in the case of the boy, some females never lose their inhibitions toward the male. He whom they cannot and dare not trust, they do not know. If circumstances place girls in an environment where they live in close contact with one another, to the exclusion of the opposite sex, they may never make the effort to know him. Instead, they may become "familiar with the familiar" in a homosexual relationship, where the body they caress is no more strange than their own, and the apparent effects harmless.

Many boarding schools breed these associations as a swamp breeds mosquitoes. Crushes on one another and on faculty members are as much a part of these schoolgirls' lives as soccer, "sings," chaperoned trips to town, pillow fights, secret midnight feasts, and finals. Needless to say, not every girl who develops a crush in such a boarding school allows her passion to culminate in overt homosexuality. Just as throughout the sexual life, in this stipulation too the power of the inhibitions plays a great part. Thanks to this, and to the power of the will, and to the chance that the love object may not respond to the lovelorn, in a great many instances a girl who for three or four years had thought and felt as a homosexual may learn to feel and think along the lines of normal sexuality when she is removed from the all-female environment. Some of her less fortunate sisters, however, once they are initiated into the practice of homosexuality, persist in it long after they have lost their class rings and forgotten the words to their alma mater. A few are never able to fight off the blight of such overt homosexuality, neither by determination, sublimation, nor psychoanalysis. For them, heterosexuality was finished in finishing school.

In the strict New England boarding school I attended during the man-scarce years of World War II, half of the teachers were paired off in abnormal relationships, as was half the student body. The night Miss Bell threw the vase at Miss Kantor and screamed out, "You couldn't be faithful to me or anyone else!" the narrow dormitory hallway outside Miss Bell's room was filled with pajama-clad girls, muffling their giggles with their bathrobe sleeves. An enterprising senior on the top floor of Old Main charged five cents a look through her opera glasses at the love affair between the gym teacher and the music teacher, going on throughout the year in the latter's quarters across the courtyard. When Miss Swanson, the math teacher, was paid a visit one week end by a husky captain in the Army, we all anticipated Miss Courtley's bad mood in science class the following Monday.

"Love that cannot speak its name!" was screaming its name in that fine old finishing school, and flashlights lit the way along darkened dormitory corridors after "lights out." If the students were well aware of the teachers' special friendships, the teachers too were enlightened as to the students'. The gym teacher, for whom I had a special aversion, frequently implored me to play a better game of hockey with the words "Go in and get a goal for Margie!" Margie, as she well knew, was "my girl." Although I was notoriously poor in sports throughout my four years at the school, upon my graduation this same woman wrote over her picture in my yearbook, "Keep up the practice through the years. You'll be a real 'pro' someday." Smiling as she handed the book back to me, she said, "I think you know what I mean."

This was the school where a girl was severely reprimanded for waving from her window at a pasting cadet from the nearby military academy, and where she was encouraged to attend "dance hour" on Saturday afternoon, during which, with her female partners, she waltzed dreamy-eyed to the lyrics of "All or Nothing at All." It was the school where the recipient of a letter from a young soldier marked "S.W.A.K." on the back was advised by the eagle-eyed headmistress to inform said soldier to omit such tawdry symbols from future correspondence; yet where passionate love notes were passed freely from girl to girl in a supervised study hall. It was the school where bimonthly early-evening visits from boys were chaperoned meticulously by purse-lipped supervisors, but where daily late-evening and early-morning visits from the girl down the hall went unheeded. This was literally a no man's land.

Here, as in countless schools like it, the development of a normal heterosexual feeling was repressed; homosexuality was permitted or ignored. By degrees, such conditions cannot fail to lead to a young girl's positive antipathy to the opposite sex. Even when nothing more has happened between two girls than petting and embracing, an insurmountable barrier can be erected between homosexuality and heterosexuality.

Krafft-Ebing, in his pioneer study of perversion, cites an example of a woman with a boarding-school background who was unable to adjust to marriage. Mrs. A., as he terms her, (Obs. 159) was twenty-six years of age, married seven years, and the mother of two children. Ostensibly she seemed to be a normal woman; however, she confessed to passionate inclinations toward persons of her own sex. Although she felt respect and a certain sympathy for her husband, sexual intercourse with him was repulsive to her. Since the birth of their youngest child, she had forced him to abstain from any marital relations. In boarding school she had already cultivated a keen interest in other young women, which she described as "love attention." She did not assume a particular sexual role in her homosexual relations, and she did no more than indulge in petting and embracing other girls. Occasionally she had also felt herself attracted to men, and once a man had aroused her sufficiently so that she avoided being alone with him for fear she might "forget herself." This, though, was a mere passing episode in contrast to her lesbian yearnings. Failure to gratify them made her painfully uncomfortable, and generally neurotic.

Here we see an inclination to normal relations blocked by a background that was permissive toward homosexuality and cultivated fear of the male. Fleeing from the warm arms of homosexuality, this young woman married a man in whose embraces she remained cold; but she feared to be alone with one who roused her, because he might have proved dangerous to her. She feared him as she feared falling in love with any man, for love of a man implies submission to him. She ran from him, not because she was unable to yield herself, but because she was genuinely afraid of him. Had she never known the love of the "familiar" and its ensuing, if only temporary, feeling of security, she might never have feared the unfamiliar to such a point that she would rather stay frigid than risk giving herself to the "mysterious" male.

Still another fear of the young female is the fear of inadequacy, with its consequent fear of not being wanted. Little girls whose parents had wanted a boy have faced and fought this fear all their lives. Again in *Sex Variants*, Dr. George W. Henry illustrates this with the case of a homosexual woman, "Myrtle K." Before she was born, a baby brother had died, and Myrtle always knew her parents had wanted another boy. While they were kind to her as she grew up, they invariably treated her as a boy, and she did her best to be like one. She learned to shoot, ride, climb trees, and play baseball, and while she would pick up snakes in her bare hands, a kitten horrified her. The image of her father, she emulated his behavior as much as possible. At thirty she gave the impression of sturdy masculinity, and in her sexual relations with women she visualized herself as a man, and she talked as if she were a man when recounting the details of her many affairs.

The young girl's fear that her sex is a disappointment to her parents was vividly portrayed for me in the person of "Pretty Nicky," a butch acquaintance of mine. Nicky, or Stella, as she had inappropriately been christened by her Italian mother, is about as masculine as a lesbian can make herself. Dressing always as a male, Nicky goes so far as to encourage the dark down of hair on her cheeks and above her upper lip by daily shaving. A handsome, husky girl, she hails originally from a modest farm in upstate New York. After her father died in Italy when Nicky was five months old, her mother brought her and her five brothers to America. As a child Nicky dressed in her brothers' hand-me-downs, and from the time she was able to walk she proudly worked alongside the boys in the fields and orchards. Lauded by her mother for contributing as much in labor and income as the rest of the children, Nicky was rewarded with a feeling of affection and security for her disavowal of her femininity.

"Stel earns as much as her brothers, and holds down the

same jobs!" her simple seventy-year-old mother brags. "And she's a good girl besides. She doesn't monkey with men!"

Pretty Nicky is one of many who have renounced their sex because their environment is such that only as a male can they feel adequate and wanted.

Some young girls who find themselves in a similar environment retain their femininity, but harbor a surreptitious resentment toward these men in whose shadows they live. Laura, a beautiful and extremely feminine lesbian I know, is on the verge of divorcing her third wealthy husband. A typical gold-digger, she rarely feels any sexual inclinations at all toward her husbands, and never feels even a remote affection toward a prospective husband whose financial assets are not considerable. She was raised during the depression years, and after her father died her older brothers received all of her mother's attention and affection. As a baby she had been her father's favorite, and he had dominated the family group. Then suddenly his death left Laura deserted. Her brothers were the breadwinners in those impoverished times, and they were always fed, clothed, and cared for by their mother before she was. Thus as she grew to womanhood she felt that the male owed her all the comforts of life, since because of him she had been deprived of them as a child. The female, her mother, who had made her feel unloved, had a debt of love to pay, and Laura had a vast reservoir of love to give in response to that female. By refusing to love the male, whom she insists must be her provider, and by seeking substitutes for him in female partners, Laura spends her life getting even with her father for dying and with her brothers for living.

In less pointed fashion than Nicky and Laura, but with the possibility of the same effects, every girl in her development knows this sense of inadequacy in relation to the other sex.

A riddle asked me by a little boy in the first grade of the grammar school I attended bewildered me for quite awhile.

"What do I have that you don't have?" was the question.

The answer was: "Outdoor plumbing!"

While the meaning of the joke was lost on me at the time, I was well aware of the "outdoor plumbing" that distinguished the male from me. By comparing her own body with that of a little boy, the little girl is bound to notice at an early age that nature has equipped him with an organ that she lacks. Freud believed that her discovery leads to what he termed "penis envy," and he viewed it as a turning point in the life of the girl.

Besides this vexation of inadequacy because of a physical deficiency, the little girl is later impressed by the social privileges connected with being a man, and the disadvantages of being a woman. At puberty comes the beginning of menstruation. The young lady feels damaged and ashamed, evidenced in her description of her period as "the curse," or her flippant statement, "I fell off the roof." Even without taking into account her physical suffering, which varies with the individual from little to great, this female phenomenon is always a source of embarrassment and humiliation to the young girl.

Soon after menstruation, this young lady, in anticipation of her first sexual experience, learns the fact that this initiation may involve a process that in some degree requires further shedding of her blood. Then finally, popular descriptions of pregnancy are filled with references to "morning sickness," peculiar desire for strange foods at odd intervals, the ugliness of the barrel-like figure and the maternity clothes that envelop it, and the likelihood that a pregnant woman's husband will prove unfaithful during the period when she is unavailable to him. She needs only to read the Bible for the icing on this bitter cake; in Genesis childbirth is described this way: "Unto the woman he said, I will greatly multiply thy sorrow, and thy conception: in sorrow thou shalt bring forth children. . . ."

A Frenchman, Michelet, in his book *L'Amour*, published a century ago, referred to woman as "*l'éternelle blessée*," translated

the "everlastingly wounded one." Freud considered it part of
her "masochistic" make-up that a woman resigns herself to,
and ultimately revels in, the aura of injury surrounding and
touching her life. And Helene Deutsch, writing in *The Significance of Masochism in the Mental Life of Women*, regarded the
female's acceptance of these "injuries," a constant factor in
female development, as indispensable to her acceptance of the
whole of her sexuality.

It would seem, then, that all women have in their lifetimes
sensed inadequacy, resentment, jealousy—call it what you
will—toward the male. To say that this or that woman has
penis envy does not mean anything. What matters is its influence on her character formation.

Whether or not she will come to an acceptance of the disadvantages of being a woman, necessary to the ultimate enjoyment of the greater advantages of being a wife and mother,
depends largely on the examples set for her by her own mother.
Psychoanalysts have put strong emphasis on the importance of
the early relations established between the homosexual woman
and her mother.

"Mother is a dirty word!" I remember one lesbian
exclaiming angrily, and in sharp contrast to that statement,
another told me, "Mom was the only woman I ever really
loved. Any other female is just second fiddle!"

Here lies the paradox of a mother's love for her daughter.
An adolescent girl finds equal difficulty in escaping her mother's
influence if she has been watched over too lovingly by a neurotic mother and if she has been maltreated by a bad mother.

In the first case, the relationship often verges on homosexuality. A roommate of mine in college, who eventually became a
practicing lesbian, was a victim of this type of all-engulfing
mother love. The father, a week-end drunk with a violent disposition, regularly raped his wife during his periods of intoxication.

"I want it and you're going to give it to me now!" My

friend remembered hearing her father's words thunder in their house early one morning, when he had come from a drinking bout. "That's what women are for!"

When the father had fallen off to sleep after such performances as this one, the mother would slip into bed with her daughter, hold her, caress her, and softly cry out her hatred for men and her love for her child. This "love" on the part of her mother was developed to the point of breast-fondling, and the first orgasm my former roommate ever had was experienced in her mother's arms.

Havelock Ellis, in the second volume of his *Studies in the Psychology of Sex*, gives a good example of the adolescent daughter who, rejected by her mother as a child, finds a substitute in an older woman, when she is in her teens. His subject described her emotion as that of an orphan who had suddenly acquired a mother, who would touch her, hold her in her arms, let her sit on her lap, and kiss her good night upon the mouth.

For the adolescent girl, the mother can be many things: a friend, a lover, a protector, an enemy, a rival. Leaving infancy behind, the little girl passes on to new personal contacts, and her father begins to play a major role in her life. She is strongly attracted to him, and she is jealous of the competition she sees in her mother. If the father is unresponsive, or appears to the child to reject her love, she may react, in order to defend herself against her thwarted feelings, by trying to be like her father.

In *A Case of Homosexuality in a Woman*, Freud reported the history of a lesbian who suffered from this feeling of rivalry with her mother, and her consequent identification with her father. During puberty, when the patient became keenly conscious of her wish to have a child, and a male one, subconsciously she was really desirous of having her father's child and his image. When, instead, it was not she that bore the child, but the unconsciously hated rival, her mother, the young girl became furiously resentful and embittered. She turned away from her father, and from men altogether, at the same time foreswearing her womanhood and seeking a female lover. In other words, psychologically she changed into a man, and took her mother as a love object in place of her father.

The Illusionist, a novel of lesbianism by Françoise Mallet, has Hélène, the teen-aged, motherless daughter whose busy father never seems to have time for her, fall in love with his mistress, Tamara. Since her father rejected her, she sought revenge by being a better man than he, and winning away from him the same woman who had caused him to be disloyal to her.

The familiar words of the old song, "I want a girl just like the girl that married dear old Dad" have an ominous ring in the mind of the lesbian.

What really makes a woman a lesbian? Fear, first. Fear of the "snips and snails and puppy dogs' tails." Fear of pregnancy. Fear of submission, penetration, and the possibility of ensuing rejection. Fear of the unfamiliar as contrasted with the familiar. Fear of inadequacy, and the fear of not being loved because of a seeming physical deficiency. The fear of rivalry and the fear of rejection.

Fear with its many faces is the first enemy to invade the childhood of a female. If her situation in that environment renders her a vulnerable target, the attack can serve to stunt her normal growth. Then the other members of fear's fraternity, resentment, envy, anger, and hatred, follow through in changing a normal girl into a homosexual woman.

The lesbian is the little girl who couldn't grow up. Whether she is a perpetual tomboy who has yet to don high heels, a silk dress, and lipstick to brave the world of grownups, or whether she is a charming and very feminine "adult child," she is an immature and abnormal woman. Her world is self-centered, and centered on her other selves. As a lesbian, she looks in an eternal mirror for a reflection of her own image, in the image of mother substitutes, child substitutes, and substitute sisters.

3.   LOOKING BACKWARD

The Moon and Pleiades have set, Midnight is nigh,
The time is passing, passing—yet alone I lie.

This lament of a frustrated lover was written some six hundred years before Christ. Sappho, its authoress, is in antiquity, if not perhaps in all time, the best-known priestess of this type of love, termed today, as it was even then, "lesbian."

The Greeks had a word for it—and it is from the Greeks that we borrowed the word "lesbian." Homosexual love among women was widely known in ancient Greece, and was allegedly introduced by Sappho on the island of Lesbos. Her fondness for associating with young and pretty women friends was compared with the love of the Greek sage Socrates for handsome youths. Legend has supposed her to be the founder of a school of female homosexuality.

However this may be, historical documents reveal that in ancient Greece, as well as in ancient Rome, long before and long after the days of Sappho, homosexuality was widely practiced among both men and women, and was not generally regarded as in any way disgraceful. Havelock Ellis, in his exhaustive work *Sexual Inversion*, gives a lucid account of this situation, and declares that ancient Greece must be regarded as a pre-eminent seat of homosexuality.

In the classical reports of the matter, homosexuality among men is mentioned much more often than homosexuality among women. This is because whatever woman's sexual, spiritual, or social role was, it was seldom considered of sufficient importance to record. Greek writers were males, and they were concerned with the male world, which was separate and distinct from the world of women. Save for the whores and the hetaerae, the female of that era was looked upon primarily as a producer of progeny. Love between male and female was virtually nonexistent. In Sophocles' writings there is no sexual love, and in Euripides it is only the women who fall in love. Theogenis compares marriage to cattle breeding, and Alcman, when he wishes to be complementary to the Spartan girls, speaks of them as his "female boy friends."

John Addington Symonds, in his study of ancient Greece, tells us that whereas the men were engaged in all the activities of public life, their wives and daughters were secluded in domestic occupations, associating mainly with slaves and knowing very little of what was going on in the outside world. The law treated them as minors. In Athens, as a rule, marriages were arranged by the parents, and a man's motive in marrying was far less the desire for a common life with a woman than the wish for legitimate offspring and a sense of duty to the country.

The hetaerae, a species of prostitutes, were probably the only women who were treated by the Greek men with a respect nearly akin to love, as we understand the word today. Distinguished from the girls of the brothel by their education and the social acceptance they enjoyed, they were apt at fascinating the most distinguished personalities of their time, from generals to statesmen.

"We have hetaerae for our pleasure," Demosthenes says in one of his speeches, "concubines for our physical needs, and wives for the procreation of legitimate offspring."

Ranked second to, if not alongside of, the hetaerae as love objects of the Greek male were young boys. Few women ever received a love note anywhere near as affectionate and passionate as this example of a typical one sent by a man to a boy, recorded in the letters of Philostratus:

> These roses desire with longing to come to you, and their leaves as wings carry them to you. Receive them kindly as a memorial of Adonis, or as the purple blood of Aphrodite, or as the choicest fruits of the earth. The crown of olives adorns the athlete; the towering tiara a great king; the helmet a warrior; but the rose is the ornament of a beautiful boy, since it resembles him in fragrance and in color. It is not you who will adorn yourself with roses, but the roses themselves with you.

The myth concerning Zeus' love for the young boy Ganymede, whom the father of the gods transported from earth to heaven because of his wonderful beauty, was sung by Homer. The poet tells us that the sensual love with which the god was inflamed toward this lad was so great that it exceeded Zeus' love for Leda, Danaë, and all the other mortal women he had known. This myth, which glorifies the passion of a god for a boy, probably helped to spread through ancient Greece the belief that there could be nothing wrong if a man should imitate the ways of the gods. It may serve to explain why the love of boys attained an especially high development in the towns where Greek civilization was most advanced, as in Athens, Corinth, and Sparta, and why it was generally approved in these cities. Many of the most noted poets, orators, and philosophers of ancient Greece have discussed this theme of the love of boys in terms that show, beyond the possibility of dispute, that these great men were devoted to the practice of homosexuality.

What, then, was the lot of the woman in ancient Greece?

We are told by Hans Licht, in his book *Sexual Life in Ancient Greece,* that she remained secluded in the gynaeceum, which was "all the rooms which formed the wife's kingdom." Only the bedroom and eating room were shared by a husband and his wife, and the latter was never available to the wife when her husband entertained friends or guests at meals. Courtesans or paramours were the sole women in attendance at those gatherings.

The domain of the wife was not the social domain. Living in great retirement as she did, the Greek female was rarely familiar with any other male than the one she married. Plutarch crystallized her situation in the anecdote he related concerning King Hiero and his spouse. Having been ridiculed by an opponent for his foul breath, the King came home in a rage and demanded to know of his wife why she had not told him of this condition.

"I thought," the modest and honest wife replied, "that all men smelled like that."

The old slave Syra in Platus' play *Mercator* comments: "My, my! Women do live under hard conditions, so much more unfair, poor things, than the men's. Why, if a husband had brought home some strumpet, unbeknown to his wife, and she finds it out, the husband goes scot-free. But once a wife steps out of the house unbeknown to her husband, he has his ground and she's divorced. Oh, I wish there was the same rule for the husband as for the wife!"

Thus, in a society where the men were so preoccupied, the women could not fail to unite and find among themselves consolation for their solitude. If less is recorded about the prevalence of homosexuality among women than is written about the same practices among men, it is because very little is said about women at all. For this reason, what we know of Sappho's life and what few remaining fragments of her poetry we have preserved for us are of unique value in offering insight into the lesbian of antiquity.

The island of Lesbos, where Sappho lived, was then the center of the world. John Addington Symonds calls it "the island of overmastering passion," and Homer refers to it in the *Iliad* as a "well-inhabited island whose maidens surpassed in beauty all the tribes of womankind." It had for its capital a city more elegant than Athens and more corrupt than Sardis—the city of Mytilene, built upon a peninsula overlooking the shores of Asia. The narrow streets were perpetually crowded with a throng resplendent in many materials—tunics of scarlet and of hyacinth, robes of transparent silk, and mantles trailing in the dust kicked up by yellow shoes. Women wore huge earrings of gold set with raw pearls, and massive bracelets of shining silver. Men and women alike wore their hair brilliantly perfumed with rare oils. The Asiatics had soft, tinted boots, and the Greeks wore sandals with the ends fastened to their bare ankles by large serpents of bright metal. The façades of shops were lustrous with the fine goods on display for sale— rugs of lush wool, cloths worked with threads of gold, jewels and ivory and amber. Mytilene was a city of the sensual, a city where the eye saw beauty everywhere.

The animation of Mytilene did not end with the day. History tells us there was no hour so late that one could not hear through the open doors the joyous hoots of the whores and hetaerae, the noise of the dances, and the high sounds of musical instruments playing for the persistent pleasure of the Mytilene men.

And what were the women up to in Mytilene? Contrary to the customs of Athens and Corinth and other Greek cities, the women of the island of Lesbos were allowed more freedom by day. Their daytime pursuits, in many instances, either compensated for or influenced the way in which they spent those nights when their men were occupied with wine and dancing girls.

A common diversion for these women was found in societies for the cultivation of music and poetry. Because such a large part of the domestic work was accomplished by slaves, women had many idle hours to spend. They joined these somewhat aesthetic clubs, and enrolled their daughters in similar seminaries, where all received musical instruction and learned in general to be more graceful in appearance and manner.

Sappho's salon, which she called her "House of the Muses," was not unique. There were others on the island, including the one a former student of hers, Andromeda, left Sappho to found, taking with her Sappho's beloved pupil Atthis.

"The thought of me, Atthis, has become hateful to thee," Sappho wrote despondently when she noticed her protégée's wavering of loyalty. "Thou doest hover around Andromeda."

Then, when Atthis did finally desert her, the bereaved teacher said bitterly, "Now Andromeda has a fair reward!" And much later, plaintively, "Once I loved thee, Atthis, long ago. . . ."

If Sappho's school for young ladies was not unique, the nature of her instruction may well have been. Aphrodite was Sappho's goddess, and Sappho made a literature of love. The Latin poet Ovid, who was fortunate to have read her poems in their complete form, declared that there was nothing more sensual than these lyrics, and added that they contained a singular course of instruction in female homosexuality. Horace labeled Sappho "the male" (*mascula Sappho*), noting that her poetry was saturated with physical, mental, and spiritual adoration of the female.

In the last chapter, mention was made of the mother-daughter quality of lesbian relationships. In Sappho we have a prime example of this. Passionate "mother" to her brood of blossoming females, Sappho herself reveals her maternal instincts in her writing.

Daughter I have with beauty's dower,
Graceful in form as a golden flower,
Darling Cleis, whose deep eyes shine
Reflecting the love that lies in mine;
And not for Lydia's land in fee
Would I trade that trust which she holds in me.

Proving too the ability of the homosexual woman to reverse her role toward her love object, Sappho wrote at another time, "As a child to its mother, so I flee to thee."

Many timid historians have tried to whitewash Sappho's relationships with her young pupils, but today only the most naïve could be led to believe that they were all innocent. The variety of Sappho's emotions is the variety an active passion enjoys, and the constancy of her mention of that passion for members of her own sex is the constancy of an unwavering love. This love kindled the multitude of moods with which all lovers become familiar.

In another lament for Atthis, we see a mood of tempestuous longing:

Atthis has not come back to me as I expected, and
	indeed I wish I were dead;
She who wept many tears as she left me, and said to
	me, "Alas, how sad our fate!
Nay, Sappho, against my will I leave thee." To her, I
	answered,
"Go away rejoicing, and remember me, because thou
	knowest how I cared for thee.
If not, I would fair remind thee of what thou for-
	getest,
That is, how dear and beautiful were the things we
	enjoyed together."

A self-pitying Sappho is shown in the lines:

For to whomsoever I do good
They harm me most.

Freudians would add that those lines also reveal a masochistic nature that perhaps nurtures the lover's injury. Indeed, Sappho may well have had that sort of personality that places itself in a position in which it is easy, if not inevitable, to suffer hurt feelings. For one of Sappho's major occupations was writing wedding songs praising the beauty of the bride and congratulating the lucky groom. These songs, composed and sung to her lyre, were taught to choruses of men and women who accompanied the wedding procession.

Sappho's envy of the male is evident in this song:

That man appears to me to be equal to the gods who
    sits before thee,
And beside him hears thee speaking sweetly, and
    laughing love's lovely laughter,
Which sets my heart within my breast aflutter.
For when I see thee but a moment, no speech is left
    in me.
Yea, my tongue is broken, and straightaway a languid
    fire has run under my flesh,
And with my eyes I see nothing; my ears ring and a
    sweat pours down over me
And trembling seizes every limb.
I am paler than grass, and appear to be dead.

We see in Sappho's poems compassion, yearning, self-pitying brooding, joy, envy, resentment, and the lover's luxury, forgiveness. To Atthis, who eventually comes back to her, Sappho says simply:

Thou hast come. Thou hast done well.
I longed for thee, and thou hast inflamed my heart
Already burning with desire.
Hail to us many times!
And for as long as we were parted from one another.

Looking backward, then, we see a society in which, if the attitude toward lesbianism was more permissive, the problems and anxieties resulting from this type of passion were not less than they are in our own era. Sappho, spokesman for this particular cult, seems as ill adjusted to her plight as any female homosexual, and at the same time as unwilling to change as are many lesbians today.

They, like Sappho thousands of years ago, are unable to resolve the question she put so well to her lover:

But let us say this, you and me—
Is it possible for mortal maidens
To be far away from the women
Whom they possess and cherish?

4.   TYPES AND STEREOTYPES

"All animals are equal," George Orwell wrote in his book *Animal Farm*, "but some animals are more equal than others."

Parodying that remark, one might say, "All homosexuals are queer, but some are queerer than others."

Within the group, types exist, and often stereotypes develop to the point of caricature. The masculine, aggressive lesbian gets a brush cut, buys a sports coat and a necktie, and becomes the stereotype butch. During a floor show in a Greenwich Village bistro one evening, a young crooner sang a sad lament that deals with this metamorphosis:

"My girl's wearing ties now,
She's changed her way.
There's no more romance
'Cause she wears the pants—
My girl's gone gay."

The butch is the caricature of the "she-man." Tough, trousered, and tart, she lives the uncertain life of the transvestite. Sometimes she is inconspicuous in society, her masquerade unknown to or ignored by her employer and her neighbors. She may or may not have a girl. She comes and goes innocuously, asking of society little more than that she be allowed to wear that male clothing which gives her some sort of strange solace. She is the venial transvestite, the benign butch—and the exception to the rule.

More often the butch makes herself conspicuous, and chooses a society in which it is safe to do so. Once she finds one of the many bohemian areas of big cities, she happily sets about the business of exhibiting herself with rapt abandon. If she works—but she probably won't if she can avoid it—she often finds employment in a night club or café that caters to homosexuals and people curious to see them. Ideally, she is kept by another stereotyped lesbian, the fem.

The best way to describe a fem is to say that she seems always to be on the verge of something. A butch is an expensive dependent, and the fem often talks of the break she is on the verge of getting, which will provide her and her lover with those luxuries for which they dare to hope.

The fem is on the verge of femininity. She too is a caricature—this time a caricature of womanliness. Her perfume is a little too heavy, her hats are a little too zany, her make-up is overdone, her walk exaggerated, and her speech affected. Her effort to be a feminine being is too concentrated. I once heard a butch whose girl friend cursed snarl angrily, "Why the hell can't you act like a lady!"

Fems try very hard to look, act, and be ladies, but they never quite succeed. If nothing else prevents the transformation, the person on whose arm they hang does. It looks, acts, and tries hard to be a man, but it is not a man. It is only "on the verge," and the difference between this person and a real man makes all the difference to the fem. She would interpret in her own way the famous French saying *"Vive la différence!"* because oddly, while she is attracted to that girl who can look more mannish than any other, she is repelled by men. A fem measures out her life in substitutes.

Some homosexuals *are* queerer than others.

Leaving the upside-down, inside-out, topsy-turvy world of the bohemian homosexual, let's focus our attention on those lesbians who "pass" in normal society.

The latent lesbian is almost legend in modern society. In novels and short stories, in plays and parlor palaver, one has become gradually acquainted with this fortyish and fiftyish female who suddenly makes an overt pass at another woman. Often she is a spinster; sometimes she is married; now and then she is a divorcee or a widow. In a moment of recklessness her hand reaches out compulsively for the forbidden fruit, and after all those years of ostensible heterosexuality she is ostensibly a homosexual.

A middle-aged female executive one night calls upon her pretty young secretary to remain after five, allegedly to "get some work out." The following day this woman is an ex-executive and the blushing but bubbling stenographer is the center of attention in the ladies' room.

"I thought I'd die when she kissed me on the neck and told me she fell in love with me the first time she ever saw me," the girl recounts her adventure excitedly. "When I told my boy friend, he said I should go right straight to Mr. Pelsner and get that lesbian out of there!"

"Who'd ever think old Gertie G. Crane was a queer!" the ladies'-room audience choruses.

This type is nearly a stereotype. Supposedly she has, up until the eleventh hour, controlled her lesbian longings, and acclimated herself well in the heterosexual world. When, sadly, she lets her libido off the string and meets her Waterloo, there is always someone around to mouth the familiar epitaph: "Who would have guessed?"

The fact of the matter is that probably few people would ever guess that the Gertie G. Cranes of the world were queers. Sometimes even the Gertie G. Cranes themselves would not guess it. For to some of these women their latent homosexuality comes as a complete surprise.

"I don't know what came over me last night!" a hostess told me her aggressive house guest apologized, after an evening during which she had wandered into the hostess' bed. "I must have been walking in my sleep!"

Not uncommonly, the latent homosexual offender is as embarrassed and humiliated by her advances as is her victim, once the spell is past.

A heterosexual acquaintance of mine, talking with me about the seemingly rare occurrence of female homosexuals "making passes" at normal women, related an experience of her own with a latent lesbian who propositioned her. My acquaintance was spending a week end in the country, visiting a couple who had been married for many years. After the husband retired one evening, as the wife and her guest sat on the back porch, overlooking a hill, and enjoying a nightcap, the wife asked the woman to go to bed with her.

"Go to bed with your husband," the woman suggested. The wife replied, "He's no good. *You* be nice to me."

Although the woman was somewhat shocked by this sudden manifestation of homosexuality in a friend she had known for years, she remained poised, and explained that the idea simply did not appeal to her. Rebuffed, the wife, who had been drinking rather steadily during the evening, left the porch and proceeded to roll herself down the hill. At various levels she halted long enough to implore the woman again to "be nice to me," until eventually it was necessary to awaken the husband in order to prevent the wife's further descent.

The day following this episode, mention was not made of the matter by the somewhat sheepish wife, and it has not been referred to since by her or the other woman. As the popular song puts it, "it was just one of those things."

In Lillian Hellman's play *The Children's Hour*, the leading characters, Martha and Karen, are supposedly falsely accused of being homosexuals by a diabolical pupil in the boarding school they run. Their reputations ruined, they discuss their plight in the final act, immediately before Martha commits suicide. Karen dwells on the unfairness of their situation, but Martha admits eventually that she loves Karen "maybe the way they said."

"There's always been something wrong," she confesses. "Always—as long as I can remember. But I never knew it until all this happened."

Another sort of lesbian is the so-called bisexual. In gay circles she is said to be "double-gaited." "Straight" society often describes her as an oversexed female, bordering on, if not actually suffering from, nymphomania. She is thought to be half and half, and often presumed to be extremely promiscuous. In the succeeding pages, she too will be analyzed further, but brief mention of her is pertinent in this discussion of types and stereotypes. For the word "bisexual" is being put into use more and more frequently among homosexuals. Most homosexuals I know claim that they are bisexuals, and a few frantically force themselves to live this double existence. It is these few that create the myth of hypersexuality and establish the stereotype.

In a restaurant one noontime, I overheard a man exclaim, "She can't be a lesbian! She's married!"

"Out in Hollywood, where I come from," his companion answered, "they not only get married and have two or three kids, but they also have running affairs with both sexes. They're just love-hungry, that's all."

The bisexual lesbian is indeed often love-hungry, not necessarily because her appetite is any larger than other females', but more often because she is allergic to all sexual food. Both women and men give her indigestion in the form of guilt; and yet, despite the consequences, she is addicted to the very thing she is allergic to. She cannot accept either sex, yet neither can she reject both. She wages an endless war against herself, on two separate battlegrounds, stopping barely long enough to nurse her wounds before, in the thick of battle once more, she inflicts new injuries on herself. Keeping fires going in both camps at the same time, she cannot help being burned. Unlike many homosexuals who simply talk bisexuality, this lesbian lives it, and dies countless times in the process.

Sisters of this stereotype are of two distinct types: the flirt and the one-night-stand adventuress. The former is a common phenomenon in gay bars and cafés, or in any circumstances where the presence of a lesbian is known or suspected. If she is patronizing a lesbian hangout, she is usually accompanied by a man. In any case, her delight is in teasing the female homosexual, with suggestive innuendoes, "accidental" caresses, meaningful glances, and general flirtation strategy. She sets the match to the curtains, and is the first one to scream, "Fire!" Her thrill is a vicarious homosexual feeling, and her defense against the threat of stigma or the possibility of involvement is a cry for help should some unknowing lesbian make a definite advance.

"You can't be nice to them!" I heard a flirt state furiously to her date after she had indignantly repulsed a butch's advance in a Greenwich Village bar. She had been engaged for several hours in rapt conversation with the butch, to the dismay of her date. "They think you're interested if you *are* nice to them."

His disgusted retort was: "If you'd ever been that nice to me, I'd think you were interested too!"

A bit more courageous, perhaps, or at any rate more curious, is the other type, the one-night-stand adventuress. She "just wants to see what it's like." Frigid, bored, lonely, naïve, neurotic, or desperate, she "allows" a homosexual to make love to her.

An English lady I know, who during the last war was a servicewoman, told me of her "first and last" experience with homosexuality. She had struck up a friendship with a sister

servicewoman who was an admitted homosexual. While her
friend never pressured her into any form of physical familiarity, she continually wooed her verbally. After a period of a year,
during which they were constantly thrown together, the lady
permitted her friend to sleep with her one night.

"I don't know whether it was the shocking monotony of
the war," she said in recounting the incident, "or just her
bloody persistence, but the whole thing was quite disagreeable. I got nothing out of it."

One-night-stand adventurers rarely get anything out of it.
Their homosexual proclivities, be they large or small, are better
realized in the anticipation of the possibility of involvement
than in actual involvement. They make the mistake of acting on
vague impulse, and the results are usually sordid to remember
for all concerned. Like the Bowery, the world of homosexuality
makes them vow "they'll never go there any more"; yet, having
been there once, they will not rapidly forget it.

Not to be confused with this type is the "one-time" lesbian who has had a homosexual experience during her life in
which there was a feeling of mutual attraction. Less the dilet-
tante, this type may have maintained the relationship for
months, even years, and then found herself fortunate enough
to return to, or enter for the first time, the heterosexual fold.
While she has had bisexual experience, she is not a bisexual, in
that her homosexual tendencies have transformed themselves
into a heterosexual nature.

In *The Homosexuals*, a book edited by A. M. Krich, Dr.
Robert Latou Dickinson, a gynecologist, reports the case a
young girl who had indulged in a passionate lesbian relationship during her teens. She and her roommate in school were
active lovers for over a year, until eventually their physical
activity subsided because of a vague feeling of harm. Without
remorse, they then became simply good friends, and still were
at the time the patient visited Dr. Dickinson. His concluding

comment is: "Happily married, comes for care in pregnancy."

Many homosexual women never have relations with other women. This type of homosexual either sublimates her desires or represses them. Those who are able to sublimate may live happy, useful lives, channeling their perverse sexual energies into creative spheres where the mental satisfaction they realize outweighs the physical frustration, or exhausts it.

The repressed lesbian has a harder time of it, for she is less aware of her abnormality. She may fight in other people what she half-consciously fears she is guilty of herself. Unable to call her sickness by name, she often finds that word on her lips in accusations against other women. The female attendant in a mental institution where I worked one summer regularly punished the women patients under her for any slight evidence of what she supposed was homosexuality. Forced to strip before her, they were whacked with a long yardstick and told by the irate attendant to "cut out this filthy lesbian love or you'll be black and blue on the behind when I get through with you." Repeatedly she attempted to exhort from them details of their suspected relationships, and often paid surprise visits to the wards late at night to see if she could "catch them in the act." Lesbianism was an obsession with her, and when, early one morning, the psychiatrist in charge was awakened by the shouts of a female patient and told that the attendant had tried to "touch her," she was promptly fired. The psychiatrist, who had been observing this employee closely, believed the patient's story rather than the one the attendant told.

"I was just passing by her bed," the attendant swore to the end, "and that crazy girl grabbed me—that lesbian!"

Weakened from malnutrition, the patient would have had trouble grabbing a kitten, much less this husky 155-pound woman.

Types and stereotypes exist in any group, some queer, some queerer. The danger of classifying the lesbian lies in presuming that a woman who seems to be a homosexual actually is one, and that a woman who seems completely feminine couldn't possibly be one.

The only way to know the lesbian is to meet the many women she is at close range; to see her against her various backgrounds, hear her sundry voices, and familiarize yourself with the diverse façades of her several lives. In the next few chapters the lesbian will be visited in her bars, her homes, her places of business, and in the haunts, houses, and habitats of her friends. Obvious at times, evasive at other times, elusive often, she will show her many selves and reveal her multiform situations.

5.   KEEP IT GAY!

"First they're curious; then they're curiosities."

This is Louie talking. Louie is the bartender in The Blue Room, a homosexual haunt off Third Street in the heart of Greenwich Village. He is referring to three teen-aged girls who have found their way here, and are seated now in a corner booth near the jukebox, sipping Cokes, whispering together as they watch the sights, and giggling intermittently.

"The one with the dark hair—the one in the middle," Louie says. "Next month she'll be one of the boys."

This is a spot catering primarily to the gay crowd, male and female, but "straight" customers are not excluded. A pair of sailors sitting at the bar, swallowing beers, eye the teen-agers.

"Jail bait!" one mutters.

His partner asks, "Who cares?"

The same song plays over and over. It is the current craze in the set, the latest disc to capture the prevailing mood of the majority. It is "Keep It Gay!," "You're Getting to Be a Habit with Me," or "These Foolish Things"—an old song with a new implication, or a new song with an old implication. For a time it will be hummed and heard, and then it will disappear, and its place of pre-eminence in the gay bars taken by another.

As the song comes to a close, you hear "Play that song again!" shouted from the back by a thin, handsome butch, wearing a single gold earring in her left ear; "Listen, Bill—c'mon up cozy and listen to the words," purred by a soft-spoken swish to his husky boy friend, as he leads him closer to the machine; and "That song! I'll go nuts!" grunted by Louie as he wipes the bar with a damp cloth.

The earring the butch sports, like the song, is a passing fad. Her name is Mark, and she could tell you about most of the whims, transient fashions, and peculiar caprices of this small Village clique over the past ten years. She could tell you how spots like The Blue Room open and close, change management, change names, change clientele, and change decor, with the fickleness of a floating crap game. She could recall the butches who used to be kings in this little microcosm, and used to sit as she sits now over a whisky at the bar, in drag, doing a little cruising until three in the morning, when her girl gets through work in an uptown night club. She could describe *their* girls; some vanished, just as the butches are, their whereabouts anyone's guess; some whores who are still around, turning tricks their pimps set up for them; some dope pushers who got "hung" on the stuff themselves, and now pedal with monkeys on their backs; and some, like Mark, "regulars," Village characters, standard items on the gay menu. Mark could tell you about Mark, and her story would take you on a grand tour of the bohemian homosexual world.

It would begin roughly ten years ago, when Mark was twenty-one and her name was Marion. Raised by two puritanical aunts in a small town in southern Missouri, she was a lonely, self-sufficient child. "Familiarity breeds contempt!" was her Aunt Edda's motto, and "A good name is better than precious jewels" her Aunt Clara's. Believing that they were a head or two above most of the families in that small community, Marion's aunts discouraged any friendships Marion seemed on the verge of forming, by reminding her "who you are." Strict Baptists, they declined to subscribe to the daily newspapers, and studied the Bible each evening, making sure that Marion memorized long passages they considered pertinent to "the good way of life."

Because there was no man in the family, Marion learned to do whatever man's work there was to be done around the house. She made repairs, cut the lawn, shoveled snow from the sidewalks, emptied the trash, and even made odds and ends like doorsteps, end tables, and chairs in a little workshop she had set up for herself in the basement. Her aunts encouraged her along these lines, for, as they often declared, idle hands are the devil's helpmate, and in addition, with Marion apt in such tasks, it was not necessary to hire a man to help out. Men, Marion had learned at an early age, were not trustworthy.

During her teens Marion dreamed of leaving the small town of her birth and escaping her aunts' rigid domination. She visualized herself living in a large city, working at some sort of job in which she could advance and become proficient, until perhaps one day she would have a business of her own. Everything about her dreams of the future was hazy and undefined, because Marion lived in the kind of cloistered environment that made any outside world seem vague and slightly unreal. The only thing she was sure of was that she would leave home as soon as she was able to, and "go someplace big."

In high school she took a course in typing, and the summer after she was graduated she got her first job, much against her aunts' wishes, in a local insurance office. Edda and Clara had small yearly incomes, and Marion did not have to contribute any part of her wages to their support. Scrupulously she saved until she had enough money to go to New York.

A tall, slender girl with a rather straight figure and a good wholesome face with regular features, Marion seemed no different from hundreds of other young girls alone in Manhattan for the first time. She found lodgings in a rooming house on West Twenty-eighth Street, and got a job as a clerk-typist on a trade publication. In her spare time she saw movies, read magazines, and went for long walks around this city that was so new to her, so huge and free and fabulous. While she made a few acquaintances at her office, it was not until three months after her arrival that she formed her first real friendship. This was with Casey, a girl who lived down the hall in the Twenty-eighth Street rooming house.

Casey had a job in a factory on the night shift, one that let her out of work at midnight. The factory was located six or seven blocks from Greenwich Village, and it was the kind of job for which one wore old clothes that could take a lot of soiling. Casey always wore slacks and a shirt, and because she was a big, husky girl, with masculine build and masculine mannerisms, the outfit suited her. Her proximity to the Village suited Casey too, because Casey was a homosexual, and midnight found her heading for the gay bars, for a few drinks before she went home to bed. During the day she slept, and just about the time Marion was coming home from work, Casey was leaving.

They met in the hallway one Sunday, several days before Christmas. As they talked together, Casey learned that Marion had no place to go for Christmas. She planned to spend the day in her room by herself. And Christmas Eve? Perhaps she would go to a movie.

"No one should spend Christmas like that!" Casey insisted, and so it was that Marion attended her first gay party, on the night before Christmas, in a Village flat with Casey and her friends.

The apartment where the party took place was a large three-room one belonging to a feminine lesbian named Lee. Materially better off than the average Village homosexual, she ran a small leathercraft shop on Fourth Street. Tony, a transvestite who lived with Lee, also worked rather halfheartedly in the shop, but like many butches in the bohemian homosexual world, Tony did not take to work with much enthusiasm. She was the "man" of the twosome, and in some gay circles the role of the breadwinner falls to the feminine lesbian. It is often hard for a butch to find a job for which she can wear male clothing, and to ask one of them to don a skirt and brave the world as a woman would be equivalent to asking a real man to do the same. Thus, even though Tony could dress as she always dressed while she worked for Lee, she was well aware of the fact that some butches did not have to work at all. *Their* girls supported them.

Tony and Lee had put up a huge Christmas tree, which everyone was helping to decorate, and a bowl of wine punch was set out on a table, along with plates of sandwiches, celery and olives, fruit, nuts, and cheese. When Marion and Casey arrived, the group was singing to the accompaniment of a lithe-looking towheaded boy's guitar. Girls were dancing with girls, boys with boys. Many of the girls, like Casey, were wearing male clothing, and there was something peculiarly feminine about all of the five young men in the room.

"I didn't know boo about homosexuality then," Mark told me when she was describing this incident to me, "but somehow I wasn't surprised or shocked or embarrassed by those kids. I just accepted them naturally—the same way they accepted me."

Everyone ate and drank too much and stayed too long, but no one regretted it, least of all Marion. Lee was particularly nice to her, and at the end of the evening she asked Marion to come back the next day with Casey for a turkey dinner. The "kids" had been warm and friendly toward Marion. Christmas was a better time because of them.

For a time, Marion and Casey traveled together in this gay set. Week ends they hung out in gay bars, and during the week, while Casey worked until midnight, Marion waited for her in Lee's shop, in the apartment Tony and Lee shared, or in a homosexual bistro. Then together the couple did the rounds of the Village spots, drinking cheap draught beer, listening to the jukeboxes and the gossip they heard around them, and mingling exclusively with lesbians. The movies, the magazines, and the long walks around New York City faded into Marion's past. Although she was not romantically involved, she was emotionally alive perhaps for the first time. She knew people; she had friends. Casey was her bosom pal, and Lee was a kind, pretty, interesting person who somewhat awed her. Often Marion helped Lee in the shop, and because of her past experience with the saw and hammer in the basement workshop of her childhood, she was an able and most willing occasional assistant. Tony tolerated her, because it meant less work for Tony.

That March, when Marion lost her job, owing to the fact that her late hours made her consistently late for work as well as inaccurate on the job, Lee came to her rescue. Lee could use an extra salaried hand in her Fourth Street business.

"It was dirty work," Mark told me. "I cut blocks of wood out on a buzz saw. After a few weeks I began wearing trousers I borrowed from Casey, and tying my hair back behind my ears with an old bandanna, so it was out of my way when I was at the machine. One day Lee took a look at me and said, 'My God, you'd make a handsome butch, Marion!' and when she put her hands up to my head to smooth back my hair, I just couldn't help myself. I grabbed her and kissed her. That was the start of everything. That was when I knew Lee was for me."

Marion had her hair cut the next day by a barber on Third Street.

She said, "When I went in there and told him I wanted a man's brush cut, he said, 'A haircut isn't going to make a man out of you, kid,' but he did the job for me. When he was finished, he said, 'That'll be seventy-five cents, sir,' and he slapped his knee and laughed. I felt like a fool, and all the way back to the rooming house I thought people were staring at me. I kept feeling my hairline with my hand, and it was like some kind of crazy dream. I didn't regret it—all I could think of was Lee and how I wanted her—but I didn't believe it, either. When Casey saw me she just said, 'Welcome to the fold. I knew you'd go butch. I saw it coming for a long time.'"

That evening Marion became Mark, and as Mark she lost her first fist fight to Tony. But the fight was all she lost. Tony lost Lee. Bad and baggage, Lee moved Mark in. Mark had a black eye, a business, and new lodgings.

Mark was twenty-two at the time. She's thirty-two now. She was a somewhat shy, uncertain, boyish butch then, eager and willing to work, still naïve about all of bohemian homosexual life, and rather overwhelmed at the facility with which she had won Lee. Perhaps this sudden revolution in her life, in sharp contrast to the unloved, overly protected, lonely, and imprisoned life she led as Marion, happened too fast to Mark. Perhaps because as a child she lived like an adult, now as an adult she became the child she never had a chance to be. Perhaps she learned to believe that only as a butch would she ever succeed in the world, because as Marion she had been a washout. Thus she must perfect her butch role; acquire toughness, invulnerability, pseudo sophistication, and always and forever new conquests. Whatever explanation there is for Mark's metamorphosis, the change in her personality is complete and awful.

Now she is a bold, pert transvestite, lazy and parasitic, no longer ingenuous in a gay world, and thoroughly confident in her conquests. Trying to prove to herself that she can love and be loved, she disproves it every day she is alive with her desperate desire to "cruise," to look always for new pastures and new prospects, because Mark is never sure inside of any kind of security with anyone.

After Mark left Lee, there was Margie, an industrious prostitute who kept Mark, and bought her a large male wardrobe and a zircon ring for her little finger. After Margie came Belle, a mulatto blues singer who filled club dates on the gay circuit from New York to Los Angeles, and gave Mark a car and a yen to "pick up on tea" (smoke marijuana). Then came Tereska, another prostitute, who cut Mark in on a percentage for pimping, and taught Mark how to read a race sheet. Tereska's friend Ginny took Mark with her to Atlantic City, where Mark learned that "horse" meant heroin, that "a hooker with a forty-pound monkey on her back" was a whore with a heroin habit, and that Ginny was that kind of whore. Finally narcotics agents picked up Ginny, and Mark went back to the Village. Now Mark goes with Evie, a chorus girl, who gives Mark an allowance and picks her up every morning around three o'clock.

"You are a stranger here but once!" One of the sailors in The Blue Room reads the printing on the back of the match folder, and, eyeing Mark at the other end of the bar, adds, "Then, baby, you're just strange!"

Some stags at the bar guffaw. Another butch, standing with a tall, dowdy-looking, red-haired fem, shoots the sailor an angry glance. "Tiny," the slim little waitress, passing with a tray of beer bottles, mutters, "If you don't like it, honey—" The swish in the corner puts his hand on his hip and squeals, "Anch-ors a-way, pet!" Louie tells the sailor that if he wants to drink here, he has to keep his comments to himself. Louie doesn't want any fights. Oblivious of all of this, Mark is watching the teen-aged trio, her back to the bar, facing them with alert, direct eyes.

"Let's meet those girls," the sailor's buddy says. "Let's go over there."

"Jail bait!" the sailor repeats, but he looks at them thoughtfully in the mirror.

The place is filling up gradually. Half a dozen lesbians occupy a center table. They are new to the Village. Most of them are butches. In their male clothing, they have an odd masquerading appearance, as though they were high-school kids still in their costumes for a school play. Their mood is one of exaggerated hilarity. They laugh too loudly, and seem peculiarly conspicuous to themselves. Their eyes dart from one another to the doorway, where they watch others like them enter.

"Got enough of everything here?" Tiny asks them.

"Ask her where the other place is," one of them whispers.

"*You* ask her."

"No, don't," the one in the middle says. "We can't ask someone who works here to tell us about another spot."

"All set here?" Tiny asks again.

"All set."

Tiny winks. "Good enough. Keep it gay!"

Mark strolls over to the jukebox, lingering there as she reads the list of selections. The teen-agers, sitting next to where Mark stands, nudge one another and glance at her. Mark is well aware of their interest.

"What'll it be?" she says to the oval-faced blonde on the end. "Got a favorite?"

Mark is wearing gray suede shoes, gray flannel trousers, a white shirt unbuttoned at the neck, and a light-blue cashmere man's sweater. She is a handsome butch, with a good profile, black wavy hair, dark eyes, a smooth, scrubbed-looking face, and a bright, lopsided grin. Her voice is deep and sure, but gentle with a practiced geniality.

"Play Number Twelve," the blonde says faintly, blushing, and Mark slips a nickel in, then turns to the threesome and stands with her drink in her hand talking to them.

"You girls sight-seeing or something?" she says. "I've never seen you in here before."

When Mark sits down with them, the sailors look at each other. One says, "Let's break it up, huh?"

"Never lost to a dike yet," his companion says.

They gulp their beers and head for the table.

"Do you like to dance?" Mark asks the blonde. The blonde is the prettiest of the three. Her long hair spills to her shoulders, and she has a sweet, angelic-looking face and a good full figure that the navy-blue skirt and white angora sweater show off well.

"I know a place we can dance," Mark says. "Not far from here, either. If you like to sight-see, you should see this place."

The fleet is in. They pull up chairs and grin at the girls. Mark ignores them, concentrating on the blonde.

"Want to go there?" she asks her.

The blonde says, "I don't know. If the others do . . ."

"My name's Mark."

"I'm Mary."

"Hi, Mary," Mark says, her dark eyes needling Mary's, until the girl confusedly lowers her glance.

"What are you *three* drinking?" one sailor says pointedly.

The other says, "If there's anyone at this table bothering you girls, there are other bars in the Village, you know. We'd be glad to act as guides."

"Maybe you're bothering them," Marks says curtly.

"If I am, baby, I'm doing it in a nice *normal* way."

Tiny serves them all another drink. Mark and the sailors drink beer, the girls Coke. The sailors pay. The banter continues, but the sailors give their attention to the dark-eyed girl on the end near them. Mary and Beth, the athletic-looking brunette in the middle, listen to Mark.

"How about it, Mary? Want to come?" Mark asks.

"If Beth would come . . ."

"I don't know," Beth says. "Can't we all go?"

"The sailors can't. No men can get in this place. It's not so far. Be fun."

"Ask Cherry if she'll go," Beth says.

"I'll get her to go to the ladies' room. I'll ask her there."

Mary taps the dark-eyed girl on the shoulder. "Want to comb your hair?"

The Blue Room is jammed now; people double up at the bar. Giggling, the teen-agers go en masse to the ladies' room. One of the sailors says to Mark, "Why don't you go home and put on a dress? Face facts!"

Mark answers, "Can't you take the competition?"

She saunters up toward the bar and back again, watching the door to the ladies' room. As she passes the center of the room, one of the butches at the table there touches her sleeve.

"Maybe you can tell us. Would you mind?"

"Tell you what?"

"We heard there's a bar just for girls. Know where it is?"

"I'm going there," Mark answers, "in just a second or two. You can follow me if you want. Isn't far."

When Mary and the others finish "combing their hair" and come out, Mary says, "All right. We'll go. Just to see what it's like. But only for one drink."

Beth says, "I'll be glad to ditch these sailors. I think they're the fresh kind."

Led by Mark, the three teen-agers start from the bar, followed by the table of butches. The sailors see them leaving. They jump and one grabs Cherry's arm in the doorway.

"You're not going with that bunch, are you?"

"Just for a while," Cherry says. "Beth and Mary want to."

"They're dikes!" the other protests. "Don't you know? They're all dikes!"

"Dikes?"

"Lesbians, honey! Lesbians!"

She pulls her arm away and the sailor grabs it again. Mark shoulders her way up to them. "What's the matter with you?" she asks the sailor angrily. "Don't you see she wants to get away from you?"

The sailor snarls, "Fil-thy les—"

"Fight starting, Louie!" Tiny calls out.

Everyone is alerted, tense. Louie comes from behind the bar, grabs both sailors by their collars. "You boys want trouble?" he says. "Want trouble?"

Mark and the others leave then. Momentarily, one sailor struggles to release himself from Louie's grip, calling after Cherry, "Wait!" Finally, seeing the impossibility of it all, he relaxes.

"We don't want no trouble," he says sullenly.

"Cool off fellows," Louie advises them. "I'll buy you a drink. Got a son of my own in the service."

The sailors nod and Louie lets go of them. Going behind the bar again, he slides two draught beers across to them. People turn back to their drinks and their conversation. Tiny takes another order. The jukebox blares.

"They were jail bait! Who cares?" one sailor says.

"Yeah. . . . They were babies!"

M's Bar is three blocks from The Blue Room. There are no lights outside, and inside it is very dim, smoky, and noisy. A large, swarthy fellow named Herb is posted at the door, carefully scrutinizing his customers before permitting them to enter. Men are not allowed, save for rare instances when a steady customer O.K.'s one. He may be a "john" who hangs around lesbians, buys their drinks, listens to their troubles, and seems to find some vicarious pleasure in fraternizing with them. Johns are usually well into middle age; many times tired, shy old men who buy themselves a seat on the side lines of this gay game, grateful for the opportunity to watch whatever minor tragedies and comedies the lesbian will perform for him in her various arenas. Sympathetic, generous, dull, and lonely, one of their kind seems always to tag along with the Village lesbians wherever they cruise.

Often the men allowed to patronize bars like M's are repressed homosexuals, who form passionate friendships with lesbians. They cannot be classified as fairies, for they are forever following girls, but the girls are lesbians. Their relationship with them is strictly Platonic, in most instances, and their acceptance of their girls' abnormality fringes on rejoicing. Not as many in number as the johns, these men are usually younger—in their twenties or early thirties—and occasionally they are married to their girls, or living with them. The marriage and living arrangement is a companionate one; they are like roommates. The lesbian stays a lesbian, and the young man drifts somewhere between heterosexuality and homosexuality.

Rarely do genuine fairies visit spots like M's. They have their own haunts, and as a rule they dislike mingling with homosexual women.

So for the most part M's clientele is female. Its life expectancy is three and a half years. The female homosexual spends less money than the male, for one thing, but if it were not for the fact that a strictly lesbian bar invites more attention than a strictly fag bar, the M's of the gay world might manage to operate longer, despite the financial situation. Not uncommonly, the location of an M's becomes infamous by the little cliques of men who hover around outside. Told by the man at the door that they cannot come in, they stand in small bands watching the lesbians enter and exit, calling out to them, and peering in at them. Eventually someone complains. The police stage a raid. The bar closes. In a week or two, at a place like The Blue Room, word goes around that there's a new M's.

"Hi, Mark!" Herb opens the door, nodding at Mark and the crowd following her. "Don't know if there's enough room back there for all of you."

But there is always enough room, and the waitress, usually a butch, gets the drink order immediately. The jukebox plays for dancing; the floor is packed with figures pressed together, barely moving, seeming only to sway to the strains of some baleful torch song.

"Dance, Mary?"

"I g-guess so."

Mark and Mary push their way into the center of the crowd. Beth and Cherry sit talking, Beth's face bright with interest, Cherry's showing a thin trace of discomfort.

"It was Beth's idea we come down here tonight after the movies," Mary says.

"Is Beth gay?"

"Hmmm?"

"Never mind. Let's forget about them for a while. Enjoy ourselves. Tell me about *you*, Mary."

M's Bar, where the whole world is gay; another no man's land, filled to overflowing with female homosexuals. The butches move through the room like little boys who are old enough to wear long pants, but too young to shave. The feminine lesbians, made up like chorus girls, flirt with them, tease them, touch the collars of their shirts with long red fingernails. Dark corners hide the hand-holders and the couples who kiss each other lightly, furtively—for even M's must know some discretion, must be wary of a possible disguised member of the vice squad in their midst. The men's and ladies' rooms are used indiscriminately. The phone booths beside them are filled with girls calling other girls, while outside those waiting in line heckle: "C'mon, my gal's expecting my call!," "Hurry it up, will you?" and "You been talking to her an hour now! Let her off the hook!"

Customers come and go; eleven o'clock, midnight. The crowd never thins out. After midnight it expands to even greater proportions. Beth is talking to two girls at the next table. Cherry watches her thoughtfully, then turns her attention to Mark and Mary, who have danced every tune.

"Want to walk with me, Mary?" Mark says.

"Where?"

"A few blocks. Over to my place. I have to pick up something. We'll come right back."

"I don't know if I should. Can Beth and Cherry come too?"

"Let them enjoy themselves. Beth is having a high old time. We'll come right back."

Cherry sees them leave and pulls at Beth's arm.

"Mary's left with that—"

"Where'd they go?"

"I don't know, but I don't like it here, Beth."

"It's all right. It's just different."

"I feel strange here. I want to get out of here."

"We can't leave Mary."

"She left us. I'm going! You can stay if you want to, but I'm getting the subway home."

Reluctantly, protesting that "you can't just leave Mary," but afraid to stay alone, Beth follows Cherry. Herb calls good night. The drugstore cowboys out front look the pair over.

"I can do anything she can do," one remarks, "better!"

"Hey, girls," another says. "What are they doing in there? They having an orgy in there?"

M's Bar at a quarter to three in the morning is at its busiest. There is a lusty "Last call for drinks!" shouted out by the butch waiters. Trays held high in the air pass through the room with double orders loaded high on them. Some feminine lesbians, still in their show clothes from uptown spots, arrive to pick up their girls. New parties swarm into the little bar, knowing M's stays open half an hour or so later than the other Village spots. The jukebox and the dancers never stop. "Last call for drinks! Last call!"

"Your friends left," Herb tells Mary when she and Mark finally return. "They left couple hours ago."

"They *left!*" She turns to Mark, near panic in her bleary eyes. "They left, Mark! Look at the time! What'll I say when I get home?" She sways a little. "I shouldn't have had that wine. Mark, ride up with me on the subway."

"I can't baby. I just can't." Mark steadies her, her arm wrapped around Mary's slim waist.

"It's only to Queens. It's— *Please*, Mark!"

"Mary, honey, I can't. Now listen, I'll walk you to the Eighth Avenue stop and put you on. You'll be O.K."

"I'm scared, Mark."

Mark hugs the girl and looks into her eyes. She says softly, "Tomorrow night we'll be together again. You'll come back, won't you? I'll call you in the morning to be sure. Don't be scared," she says. "You're not—sorry, are you?"

"N-no," Mary whispers. "Just scared."

"Will you come down tomorrow night?"

"I'll try."

"I'll call you," Mark says. "Tomorrow. I'll put you on the subway now. You'll be O.K."

As they pass Herb in the doorway, Mark draws him aside. "Listen, Herb. When Evie gets here, tell her I ran around the corner for a sandwich. Tell her I'll be back in a second. Tell her wait. And Herbie," she winks at him, "don't tell her about this."

"Mum's the word." Herbie grins slyly. "Nice doll!"

"You're telling me?" Mark smiles.

"Last call! Last call!" echoes out in the early morning air. As Mark and Mary start toward Third Street, Mark takes her hand.

"You two going to get married and have a family?" a smirking bystander in front of M's calls after them.

Mark presses Mary's hand gently. "Don't mind him, honey," she says. "He's some kind of wise guy. There are a lot of 'em down here."

6.   GAY PARIS

"So long as Paris exists," Nostradamus predicted in 1555, "there will be gaiety in the world."

Doubtless this famed French astrologer did not refer to homosexuality; yet Paris, perhaps more than any other city in the world, has accustomed itself to the existence of the homosexual in its midst with relatively little furor. Many of its leading literary lights, to whom Parisians, as well as all Frenchmen, point with pride today, have concerned themselves with the problems of the homosexual. André Gide, Pierre Louys, Marcel Proust, and Colette, to name a few, have dwelt upon this abnormality in many of their novels, poems, stories, and plays. Cafés catering to homosexuals and those curious about them are often advertised in the newspapers and the English-language guidebooks.

In *Paris after Dark*, by Art Buchwald, European columnist of the *New York Herald Tribune*, we find the following entry:

> LE MONOCLE—60 Blvd Edgar-Quinet—DAN. 41-30 A bit of Greenwich Village; masculine-looking women dancing with feminine-looking women. Music is on the corny side, but it's a possibility if you like that sort of thing.

One would, perhaps, wonder why Mr. Buchwald uses the

phrase "a bit of Greenwich Village" to suggest the existence of homosexuality in a Parisian night club. Presumably the explanation lies in the fact that this pamphlet is directed to the American tourist in Paris, and the very name "Greenwich Village" is often erroneously considered synonymous with homosexuality.

As American tourists, then, let us visit Le Monocle, and compare The Blue Room and M's Bar with this gay bar in gay Paris.

Le Monocle is located on the Left Bank, in Montparnasse. Boulevard Edgar-Quinet is a wide, long street, and this bar would look small and inconspicuous on it were it not for the taxis lined up near it. It is a Saturday night in Paris, at the end of May—an ideal time for the tourist. Le Monocle specializes in the tourist trade, and as we enter we note the sign hanging in the window: "Joyeux Cabaret—Dancing."

Apparently they are used to Americans in this Paris, and the single English word "Dancing" might suggest that they would like to cater to English-speaking people. Indeed, as we fumble for a way of saying we would like a table, the thin young man in the shiny black suit who greets us as we enter flashes a brilliant smile and says, "*Bon soir!* How do you do! Welcome!"

Le Monocle consists of two rooms; one wide and large, with a bar, a small bandstand, and a square, compact space for dancing; the other long and narrow, lined with round tables covered with white cloths. It is dimly lit, smoky, and noisy, much as M's Bar is, but a few men are present, and it is less crowded than M's. The jazzy-sounding music emanates from a four-piece band, and the M.C., standing to one side of the bandstand, is a butch. Unlike the butches in the commercial gay world of Greenwich Village, these wear straight tailored skirts instead of trousers, with matching tailored jackets, white men's shirts, and neckties. Their hair is cut boy style, their faces are not made up, and their gait and stance are masculine.

Our table is in the large room. Champagne is required. We do not require it, but it is a house rule that every occupied table in Le Monocle must bear a bottle of champagne. After our waiter, a medium-sized, solicitous Frenchman in a worn black dinner jacket, takes our order, we gaze about us.

On the dance floor are six or seven couples. One of them is a man and woman, tourists like ourselves. The others are fems and butches. At the bar are three unaccompanied men: a French soldier, a sleek-looking, greasy-haired middle-aged man, an innocuous inebriate. In addition there are half a dozen butches, their stools swung around to face the dance floor, glasses of red wine in their hands. Another party of obvious sight-seers enters and is immediately whisked to a table near our own. The music blares forth, and the voice that speaks to us suddenly must shout above it.

"'Allo. 'Ow are you zis eve-ning?"

Beside our table stands one of these masculine-looking lesbians, a large, smiling girl dressed in a navy-blue tailored jacket and skirt, a white broadcloth shirt, and a bright-red tie. She has black hair, which is slicked back straight, and a square face with sharp features, a ruddy complexion, and shining oval-shaped blue eyes.

"My name," she says in halting English, "iz Vance."

Vance sits down with us, and when the waiter brings the bottle of champagne, we ask for another glass for Vance. Instantly she protests, telling us that she will order her own bottle. We try out our French on Vance, and we learn that she lives in Paris, that she is thirty-two, and that her girl friend works in the chorus line at a night club called Eve on the Place Pigalle. Together they share a flat a few blocks from Le Monocle.

"Ve hope someday to go to Ah-merica," she tells us, "bot on-ly to vee-sit. Nut to stay."

Vance tells us that she has heard that Senator McCarthy

arrests homosexuals. America would be all right, she states, if it were not for that.

In the midst of this conversation, there is a drum roll, and the M.C. steps to the bandstand and holds her hands up for silence. When the room is respectfully still, she explains in rapid French that Le Monocle is proud to present its star attraction, Claude, a singer. With another drum roll and a great round of applause, a very startling figure steps from behind the scarlet curtain. Claude is a woman, but one would never know it if she were not wearing a skirt. Above the waist, Claude is a natural double for Cornel Wilde. She has a handsome face, bordering on prettiness, yet with nose, eyes, and mouth that seem more a man's than a woman's. Her shoulders are broad, her waist is narrow; she has a boy's build, straight and hipless. Still there is one thing left to startle us further about Claude. When she sings it is impossible to believe that her voice is a woman's.

"Claude could fool all," Vance whispers to us, and as we sit back and listen, we must agree that Claude is one of the most masculine women we have ever seen or heard.

There is more applause, and there are encores, but eventually the M.C. calls out. *"C'est fini!"* and Claude is relieved. The dancing resumes, and Vance asks us if we would mind dancing with her.

"It is on-lee sport-ing," she encourages us, smiling, "in a place like Le Monocle."

We protest that we do not feel like dancing, and petulantly Vance tells us we have hurt her feelings. She explains that she had only in mind to please us, and not to offend us. If it would offend us so—then, *well* . . . She shrugs her shoulders in a gesture of forlorn helplessness. Of course it does not offend us, and we accept her invitation. With expert grace she maneuvers us around the small area reserved for dancing. It is more crowded now. Three or four more parties of tourists have arrived. We see a Texan in a ten-gallon hat, blushing and guffawing as a butch leads him while they dance. At intervals he waves and calls to a stubby woman wearing a flower-splotched jersey dress and a feathered hat, also, somewhat nervously, dancing with a butch. We remark to Vance that the butches seem particularly keen to dance with the tourists, and Vance replies, "It is ze custom in Paris to make the foreigner feel his home." She adds that the tourists come to Le Monocle for surprises, and they would be disappointed if attention were not paid to them. When we inquire why there are so many more masculine lesbians in this bar than feminine ones, Vance answers that the girls usually work evenings. "Like mine," she adds proudly.

After our dance, and after we have watched others dancing and finished our champagne, we decide to leave. The beaming waiter presents us with our bill on a silver tray, and as we scan the items, we note a rather large charge for "entertainment." Unwilling to believe that the band and Claude could have cost us so much, we question Vance. She answers that we must not embarrass her this way, and she leaves our table. It is then that we notice that we have also been charged for two bottles of champagne—our own and Vance's. Somewhat peeved, we demand an explanation of these charges from our waiter. Vance has disappeared from view.

"But she was your guest at your table," the waiter insists, "and you bought her the bottle of champagne."

We note that the bottle under discussion has had only one glassful poured from it. The waiter continues to shrug his shoulders. He is sorry, but . . . Not wanting a scene, we agree to pay for Vance's champagne, but we still do not understand the high charge for entertainment.

"She entertained you, did she not?" the waiter asks us. "She *sat* with you."

"But we never asked her," we say somewhat indignantly.

"She danced with you." The waiter is deaf to our protests.

He repeats over and over, "She sat with you. She danced with you. She is an employee of Le Monocle. She cannot go without salary. She has entertained you."

Because eventually it becomes impossible to argue with him further, and because the situation does have its amusing aspects, though the joke is on us, we pay the bill and leave Le Monocle. Vance never reappears to wish us good night, but the same man who greeted us and showed us to our table when we first arrived sees us out the door, and calls after us cheerfully, "*Bon soir!* Come again! *Bon soir! À bientôt!*"

Le Monocle is not a typical bar for the gay Parisian. It is a tourist trap, designed for the curious who can afford to finance their curiosity. Like many Parisian façades, Le Monocle exists purely to capitalize on many foreigners' belief that Paris is a wide-open city where anything goes. The deft Parisian café-owner knows well the trick of luring the tourist with promises, teasing him with provocative stage sets and characters, and in the end taking from him his highest expectations and his newly purchased francs.

But what of those cafés that *do* cater to the gay Parisian? They are not easy to find. They are not centered in one locale, nor are they inclined to admit the outsider. The one I visited in 1954 was located in the rather unpretentious Trocadero Quarter. Downstairs in a somewhat dank cellar, it was lit by candlelight. There was no band and no jukebox, only the very soft music made by a small, dark-haired accordionist seated in a corner of the large white-walled room. As she played, she sang in muted tones, and there was none of the hilarity of The Blue Room, M's Bar, or Le Monocle. The only man present was the owner, a pleasant-faced, robust French fellow everyone called Jock. Dancing was not permitted, and few of the couples sitting at the small tables seemed to want to dance or mingle with the rest of the clientele.

This café, frequented exclusively by lesbians, is, in my

experience, exceptional for its subdued atmosphere as well as its subdued clientele. The young girls and older women whom I saw there were little inclined to brand themselves as specific fems or butches. While several of them wore pants, these pants were more like slacks than like trousers. They fitted tightly, and clung to the curves of the women's bodies. Instead of men's shirts, they favored women's blouses, usually silk or nylon ones, which showed their busts well. Most of these slack-clad lesbians also wore lipstick and perfume and powder. Outside of these surroundings I think none of them would deserve the second look the pants-wearing lesbian sometimes receives from the alert observer.

Those women in that cellar who were not wearing slacks looked quite like women one would see anywhere in "nice" society. There was none of the harsh, whorish quality about them that some feminine lesbians who frequent homosexual dives have. They seemed to possess mild natures, posed countenances, and pleasant dispositions. There was less ostentatiousness evidenced in their choice of wardrobe, fewer bright colors and bold, dramatic designs. They seemed to play everything down; to have acquired that certain sophistication that only simplicity can achieve.

As couples, these women gave more attention to each other than most of the lesbians in the Greenwich Village bars. They spoke softly together, or sat side by side sipping their drinks, listening to the accordion playing in the background, and watching one another's faces in the candlelight. There were no outward demonstrations of mutual affection; no perpetual caressing, merely a slight touching of hands now and then, and no kisses being stolen shyly in the shadows.

I was taken there by an English girl who had been studying medicine in Paris for some three and a half years. An overt homosexual herself, she had many friends both gay and straight.

"When I am lonesome for my own kind," she told me, "I

come here. Not to look for an affair. That isn't done here. But more to meet people who, like myself, are lesbians. It is relaxing sometimes just to sit and talk here with them, and listen to Lili play."

"Are there many places like this in Paris?" I asked.

"Few. I know of only one other for women, and one for men and women. The rest are all very commercial and disgusting to me."

We discussed the social diversions for the less obvious type of lesbian in Paris, and she told me that for the most part there were few parties and gay gatherings in private homes.

"I can't tell you," she said, "what the very rich homosexual men and women do for diversion. I hear all sorts of things about wild parties and orgies, but one always hears such rumors. I only know that for people like myself, who live in apartment houses and have respectable occupations, we seldom gather as a clan at home. Often we come here, but more often we do things with the person to whom we're attracted, the two of us alone."

"Could you make a rough guess at the percentage of lesbians in Paris?" I asked.

"Heavens, no! Who could do that? It's like London—you know your own circle of friends, and that's all. You hear about other circles like yours, but you only know your own—maybe ten or eleven homosexual women."

Toward midnight the crowd in the cellar—if it could be called a crowd, there were no more than twenty-five or thirty women present—began to thin out.

"It's very late," my friend observed.

I answered that it was only a quarter to twelve, and that it was a Saturday night.

"The Métro stops running at midnight," she answered. "Then it becomes difficult to get home from here. We'd better run along."

My visit to this cellar in gay Paris was a pleasant surprise. Lesbian bars, on the whole, are neither pleasant not surprising.

Gay life for the female homosexual, as lived in the gay bars and cafés of the world, is a lonely, harassed, and depressing life. The habitués of these haunts seem somehow haunted themselves—haunted by the vision of their old age, haunted by the necessity to prove their youth, haunted by their rebellion against a society that scorns them, and haunted perpetually by their strange reflection in the wide mirror over any and every bar at which they drink. If the cellar in Paris that I glimpsed briefly does truly prove to be the exception to the rule, trust Paris to produce it.

7.　　　　　　　　　　　　　COCKTAILS AT KITTY'S

Male homosexuals seem to enjoy giving and attending parties for their own kind, and most of them have a large circle of male homosexual friends with whom they gather at each other's homes. Such parties are apparently an important part of the male homosexual's life, in sharp contrast to the female homosexual's. For I think, even as my English friend observed in the last chapter, that the average female homosexual, as distinguished from those lesbians who "cruise" and cavort primarily in gay hangouts, does not "gather with the clan" very often, if at all. Many times she knows no other homosexual than the one with whom she is involved. Frequently she deliberately avoids making the acquaintance of others like her, preferring to live in society as inconspicuously and discreetly as possible. Parties consisting solely of homosexual women, outside the world of gay bohemia, are a rarity. More commonly, in my experience, lesbians meet socially at "mixed" parties, where the guests are both gay and straight. Of the few I have attended like this, Kitty's are by far the most fabulous, if not the most revealing telescopes with which to view this segment of gay society

The time is the present. The place is Sutton Place, New York. The hour is six o'clock. Kitty and Eric are giving another cocktail party for their intimate friends. Sutton Place is, by New York standards, not merely a good address, but a very good address. The apartment building in which Kitty and her brother Eric live resembles, with its many box balconies jutting out from its smooth façade, a chest of drawers with all drawers open. Kitty and Eric occupy a huge nine-room flat on the fourteenth floor. Both are successful professionals in the interior-design field, and both are homosexuals.

At the door, Kitty greets you. She is a striking woman in her late thirties, with long, coal-colored hair, a fresh and fair complexion, large green eyes, a small regular nose, and wide curving red lips. An olive-green silk hostess gown enhances her full figure. Kitty carries herself well and has a rather brisk manner. Inside the narrow foyer leading to the living room Eric stands, a tall, erect man in his forties, with dark hair that is graying at the temples, a thin, sunken face, huge round brown eyes, a high forehead, and sharp cheekbones. He combs his hair forward instead of back on his ovoid head.

"Go along in," Kitty says. "You know everyone."

Eric smiles and calls you "doll," his fingers touching your elbow as he guides you into the crowded living room. The room is so spacious that it has a somewhat cool and bare look, cultivated by Eric's and Kitty's decor. Everything is gray. The furniture is blond Swedish modern, with a huge kidney-shaped marble-topped coffee table dominating the room, and wing chairs set about it. There is a long black velvet divan, box-shaped and narrow, along one wall. Above it is hung the work of a cubist painter, a cold but colorful combination of spheres, cylinders, cubes, and parallels in various bright shades. Built-in bookcases fill the opposite wall.

"Olivia's here alone," Eric whispers. "Roddy's in another of his moods. Won't see anyone. Hasn't for *days*."

Eric is a great gossip; his hobby is intrigue.

You say hello to Olivia, who has just baptized the thick gray carpet with a dripping sauce-covered shrimp she has dropped.

"Oh, now damn!" she hoots in a hoarse and unbelievably husky voice. "Now damn it all. Now, Eric, *look*. Look what I've gone and damn done to your *rug*. Hate me!"

A maid in a gray cotton uniform rushes over and scoops the shrimp up with a paper napkin.

Eric slips away and Olivia tells you she's worried about Roddy. His face was "the color of these walls when I left him." Olivia directs a touring modern-dance group, and her homosexual husband, Roddy, is one of the performers. Olivia is gay too, but she is seldom attached to any one woman, and doubtless has more Platonic friendships with her young dancers than overt homosexual relationships. She claims that she is "too old for all that now," and she admits to forty-two. Roddy is in his early twenties. Their attachment has a mother-son flavor to it, and Olivia's chief delight in life seems to be in soothing Roddy's broken spirits after he has had a disappointing emotional experience.

A moon-faced young boy plays "The Man That Got Away" on the baby grand in the next room, while two women sip martinis and stand watching him. They are a standard threesome in this set: Miles, the piano-player, performs nightly in a club in the Fifties; Jan, his wife, is a buyer for a Fifth Avenue dress shop, traveling to Europe twice a year; and Phyllis, Jan's girl friend, is a singer with a name band. The three live together. Miles claims he is not a homosexual. Jan and Phyllis never do anything to discourage the idea that they are homosexuals. Seldom at odds with each other, the three seem quite content with life as they live it.

Kitty flits by and screeches at you, "My God, haven't you got a drink yet, dear?" and instantly Jennie appears with a tray of Manhattans and Martinis. Jennie is Kitty's maid, but she is more than a servant. She is Kitty's confidante, Kitty's scapegoat, Kitty's protégée, and often Kitty's boss. She is a small, slender Irish girl whom Kitty discovered in a Dublin inn and imported into the United States. About twenty-five, Jennie probably knows Kitty better than Kitty knows herself, and invariably Jennie dislikes the women to whom Kitty is drawn.

Currently Kitty claims to be in love with her new assistant, a somber-looking, white-faced Viennese girl who has worked for Kitty approximately six months. Attractive and talented, she is very young for this set, not quite twenty-three. Her name is Anita, and when you ask Jennie if Anita has arrived yet, Jennie snaps, "Of course. She's over there with one of those she's always mooching around."

"One of those" is an extremely feminine sandy-haired young man, sitting with Anita on the velvet couch. Anita seems to be fond of this type; often she is more attentive to these young men than to Kitty.

You go over to greet her.

Anita is tall, with broad shoulders and large hands and feet. Her figure is girlishly ripe, her face soft and lovely, though nearly always remotely melancholy-looking. She wears her auburn hair close-cropped, but combed in feminine fashion, and her fine profile carries the coiffure well.

"Bertie's telling me about an article he wrote," Anita says to you. "It's called 'I live in My Kitchen.' It's about his new apartment. It's one huge room on Central Park South, and when you push buttons, it converts into a beautiful kitchen— the stove here, the sink over there, the refrigerator here— everything you could want. Then another push of the buttons and it all slides back into the walls and you have a gorgeous living room again."

Bertie is a friend of Eric's, also in the field of interior design. He and Anita and Kitty and Eric often attend the theatre together, have dinner out as a foursome, and go to parties as a group. As you listen to their conversation you recall the evening you and Anita discussed the subject of homosexuality, and Anita told you that while she always seemed to be "involved with a woman," she had never loved a woman, or a man.

"Respect, yes," she had said, "but I don't even know love. I don't even enjoy the physical with a woman, and I have never been with a man. Men intimidate me, somehow. Real men do. I feel comfortable with the fairy boys. I like them."

Anita's childhood was spent in war-racked Germany. Her memories of her early teens are jumbled recollections of bombings, evacuations, food scarcity, fleeing, and a lonely kind of unwanted freedom to shift for herself. Separated from her only remaining family, a younger brother, Anita met a girl a little older than herself, and together they traveled from place to place to place, sleeping on park benches many times, working at odd jobs, and looking out for one another. Anita was fifteen then, the other girl seventeen. They were "like twins," Anita had said, "inseparable and afraid to be out of each other's sight." When Anita's friend had initiated a physical aspect into their relationship, Anita responded.

"She was so much a part of me, and in a way, I think I did love her—but more like a sister. Not romantic love."

Homosexuality entered Anita's life in stocking feet, so that she was barely aware that it had come to her, or that it was there at all. It was quiet, comforting, undemanding. The relationship ended much as it had started, in a natural, seemingly inevitable way. D-day ultimately brought about the girls' separation, as allied forces stepped in to organize German civilian life, and while the pair did write every day at first, after a while their correspondence diminished.

"I guess I was so used to having a girl heal my wounded spirit and keep me from loneliness," Anita said, "that a year later when I met a girl in my office who got interested in me that way, I just fell in with her. I liked her very much. She was all I knew. I wasn't used to men, and there weren't many around at the time, except the GI's, who couldn't date us.

Anyway, we were wary of them. They always seemed so sure of themselves."

The room is filling up. You say hello to Linda, a pretty and nervous redhead who chain-smokes and takes Cuddles, a miniature pinscher, wherever she goes. You congratulate her on her television performance a few weeks ago. A dramatic actress of highly emotional roles, Linda lives with Lil, an executive in the casting department of a Madison Avenue advertising agency. Linda is twenty-nine, in her third year of psychoanalysis, and one of those almost alcoholic people who get a little tight nearly very day, but who swear rather proudly that they have never yet wanted a drink when they got up the next morning. Beside Linda stand Lil, holding Cuddles. Lil is in her mid-thirties. One would probably describe her as a handsome woman, with graying hair, an athletic build, well-tailored clothes, and a kindly, warm personality.

Sid and Louise are there; both are fashion photographers. They are not homosexuals, but are great friends of Eric and Kitty. Married some nine years, they live on Long Island, and their parties are almost always predominantly gay.

"All our friends seem to be a little queer," Sid often comments. "It makes us feel as though there were something wrong with us."

Ted, a dancer with the New York City Ballet, is in a corner with Artie, his current boy friend, a silk-screen designer. As you walk by them, Ted winks and says, "Don't mind us, dawling, we're having a little family scrap."

"Whenever you get out in public," you hear Ted resume the quarrel as you go on your way, "you act simply *bitchy*!"

Eric is chatting now with Alissa, a French girl who is a buyer for a Paris department store, and a friend of Jan's, Miles's wife. She is showing him her slip, a fine black lace one.

"It is new," she says. "The new style."

"Is it a slip?" Eric says.

"Yes, a *sleep*."

"It's asleep?" Eric laughs. "Oh, doll!"

"No, no—a sleep. A *sleep*."

Phyllis is singing in the other room, while Miles plays, and Jan stands by watching her affectionately.

Jennie serves you a third drink, and from the foyer you hear Olivia's throaty voice as she speaks on the telephone.

"Roddy, I *knew* you'd be gloomy if you stayed home. Now you *are* gloomy. It's depressing for me, Roddy. Goddamn him, love, he's not *worth* it! He's nothing, Rod. *Noth*-ing!"

Kitty is sitting on the velvet couch now between Bertie and Anita, smoothing Anita's skirt, telling her she must smile and not look like such a dark cloud.

"My God, will you pay attention to what I'm trying to de-*scribe*, Kitten?" Bertie says exasperatedly. "A month from now you'll accuse me of being secretive about the design. That's the way it always happens, just when I start—"

"Honey, love," Kitty touches his face with her hand, "'Nita's blue, baby. I don't want her to be blue."

"I'm not blue." Anita sighs.

"You're blue, sugar. I know when you're blue."

"When are you and Lil going to take a well-deserved week end off," Louise asks Linda, "and come out to the Island for a visit with us?"

Linda is tight. "Cuddles comes too," she says. "Hmmm?"

"Sure Cuddles comes." Sid grins.

"Cuddles is a goddamn child substitute," Linda says.

Lil moans, "Oh, God, please! Don't start! We left Sigmund home, honey. 'Member?"

"Well, Cuddles *is*!" Linda protests. "He is a child substitute, an' I'm going to take the li'l pookie and put him right down on that big black couch down over there and psychoanalyze him."

A few more people arrive; Jill, a divorcee who collects a

sizable alimony from Hugh, her ex-husband, whose sister she fell in love with and lives with now. "Pattie couldn't come," she tells Eric. "Got a goddamn virus of some kind. Whole family is susceptible to anything going around. Hugh used to get a cold if he looked at an advertisement for cough drops."

Dwight, an osteopath, there for the first time, is Eric's newest interest. In the background of the party, as Eric rushes to meet him, clamping his arm around his shoulders, Bertie says petulantly, "So *that's* Prince Charming. La-de-*da*!"

"Don't worry, Bertie," Kitty says. "You know Eric. He's not serious."

"Kitten, you're confused," Bertie answers. "I wouldn't care if he *were*."

Jim and Ned arrive. Jim is a pale-faced young artist, Ned a political reporter. With them they bring Sandy, a woman in her thirties who writes a shopping column for a syndicate.

"Make sure everyone gets a drink, Jennie," Kitty tells the girl.

Cocktails at Kitty's—six o'clock, seven o'clock, eight o'clock. Not too different from any cocktail party, ostensibly.

Someone at a cocktail party always monopolizes the phone:

"I'm worried about you, Roddy, that's all. Love, I'm a-*fraid* for you. I have to keep calling. Now damn, Roddy, love, I'm all de-*pressed* about this!"

Someone at a cocktail party always becomes quarrelsome:

"Of course I dislike washing our linen in *pub*lic, Art, but it *does* seem to me that you're just too, too self-important for little old Theodore this night!"

Someone at a cocktail party always tells a French joke:

". . . and they were having a—how you say it in English when there's *three*?" Alissa asks Sid.

"Like you say it in French, *ménage à trois*."

"Yes! And this Englishman who was a homosexual said to the Frenchman—"

Someone at a cocktail party always becomes overly affectionate:

"'Nita, 'Nita, you're so pretty! I could just—"

"Kitty, don't. It's embarrassing."

"No, baby, these are our friends. They know I love you, 'Nita."

Someone at a cocktail party always leaves in a huff:

"But I thought we'd all go out for dinner together after, Bertie."

"Go with Dwight, lover-boy. Let him cast *his* magical spell over you. I have other eyes, Eric, old man."

And someone at a cocktail party always has too much to drink:

"Is she all right?" Sid asks Louise, his wife.

"Yes, I think so. Lil's in the bedroom with her. She knows how to handle her when she's like that."

"Well, good Lord, are you stuck with Cuddles for the rest of the evening?"

"Looks like it, honey. I inherited the baby."

Cocktails at Kitty's—not too unlike other social gatherings along Sutton place. The apartment is spacious, the furnishing fashionable. The drinks are typical, the effect on the various guests the same. The faces you see there are faces you would see anywhere in a crowd. The songs Miles plays are songs anyone might hum. It's just another get-together, like many, many others going on all over Manhattan at the same hour. The only difference between the others and this one, perhaps, is that cocktails at Kitty's are always just a little gayer.

8.   DISCRETION

"I am not joking. I'll bet you that within twenty years the words 'unnatural' and 'perverted' and so on will never be taken seriously. . . ."

These words, written by André Gide in *Corydon*, a novel in defense of homosexuality, were first published in 1924. Needless to say, they proved to be more hopeful than prophetic. Homosexuality is still a stigma, and to the vast majority of practicing female homosexuals who desire to adjust to their environment, discretion is still the better part of love. For as Gide also observed in the same novel, "We are never so isolated in life that the mud that some people sling at us does not, at the same time, spatter others who are dear to us."

The Marks of Greenwich Village, the Vances of Paris, and the Kittys of Sutton Place often set themselves up as targets by refusing to yield to public opinion and mask their abnormality. They are often the exceptions and the extremes. More often the lesbian cannot afford, economically, socially, or emotionally, the luxury of complete abandonment.

During my college years at a large state university, an example of the high cost of indiscretion in a homosexual relationship was illustrated for me in the tragic experience of two female instructors. On the surface, the only thing that made these two young women in any way different from other women at the university was the fact that everyone liked them. Both in their late twenties, they were nearer the age of the average collegian than were most of the other faculty members, and they enjoyed immense popularity among the students, who chose them for friends, confidantes, and advisers. The older professors and their wives were inclined to feel protective toward them, and frequently invited them to dinner, bridge parties, and tea. At various university functions, they would be seen with their dates, young professors in some instances, bachelor businessmen from town in others. Their lives seemed wholesome, busy, and well rounded. Their personalities were vivacious and happy.

Because they were saving for a trip to Europe during the summer vacation, they settled for the most meager accommodations in the small town where the university was located. They lived together in a large double room several blocks from the campus, rented to them by a purse-lipped old widow, whose room was directly opposite theirs in the small wooden frame house. One evening very late the old woman heard the pair arguing, and as she listened more carefully she heard the subject of their debate. It was pure jealousy, inspired by the fact that one of the young women had stayed out past midnight with a man. Her roommate flung at her accusations of "two-timing," "disloyalty," and "double-crossing," the kind a husband might shout angrily at an unfaithful wife. The quarrel, it was easy for the landlady to figure out, was a lovers' quarrel.

Highly indignant that she should be renting a room to two lesbians, the irate woman discussed the situation with her neighbors. Everyone to whom she spoke agreed that it was an unwholesome situation, and, in view of the young instructors' positions as counselors to young people, a dangerous one. The two became the objects of concentrated attention on the block, and nightly the landlady kept her ears open for "suspicious sounds." Each day there was a new development for her to report.

The rumors spread like a grass fire in a dry August, and subsequently word reached the dean of women. The suspect pair was invited for tea at her office. On the day following, substitute teachers took their classes while they packed their bags. Their resignations were explained in official terms as "resulting from nervous strain," but few were fooled. The grapevine in a small university town is more effective than the daily newspaper in relaying current events. Clichés like "Who would have thought it?" "What a pity!"; "Where'll they go now?" and "It's too bad it couldn't have been kept quiet" were on everyone's lips, and the word "lesbian" had a suddenly sharp, sad, and cruel sound to most people's ears.

Dismissing for the moment the obvious social and economic reasons for discretion on the part of the lesbian, let us focus attention on the more subtle emotional and psychological reasons.

Popeye's cocky proclamation, "I am what I am and that's all that I am" might in many lesbians' consciences be parodied as "I am what I am and I hate what I am!" For such lesbians, discretion is not only an outer defense with which to fortify their sense of security and self-respect in the community; it is also an inner defense with which to stave off their perennial pangs of guilt. These females who embrace homosexuality while at the same time despising themselves for it are in the position of that perplexed man who allegedly remarked about his wife, "I cannot live with her. I cannot live without her."

"I love Helen," Pam, a homosexual who shares an apartment in Chicago with her girl friend once said to me, "but at least one night of every week end I have to go out with a man. Not because I'm attracted to men—I never have been—but because I feel better about everything. I don't feel like such a freak. Besides," she added, "it wards off suspicion. It's the only discreet way to live in society as a homosexual, and I hate indiscretion."

Helen and Pam perhaps personify a majority of lesbians' interpretation of "discretion." Helen is in her early thirties, and works as manager of a radio station in Chicago. A personable, fairly attractive woman, she is the stronger personality of the two, often playing the role of mother to Pam's role of the child. Born and raised in East St. Louis, Helen never had the money for college, and partial support of her bedridden mother was shared by Helen and an older brother. From a job as a file clerk for a company that manufactured paper bags, Helen eventually worked her way up to her present position. Her mother's death brought her complete independence, and at the age of thirty she met Pam. Neither had ever had a homosexual experience. They were introduced at a fund-raising benefit co-sponsored by Helen's station and the small advertising agency for which Pam worked as an assistant copywriter.

"I knew Helen for a year," Pam told me, "before I knew exactly what it was I felt for her. During that year all I knew was that I wanted to be with her more than I wanted to be with anyone else. It was like being a little high all the time, and she was the liquor—and I had never felt so intoxicated with anyone in my whole life."

Pam's and Helen's relationship matured to overt homosexuality shortly after they took an apartment together. Pam was twenty-four, a recent graduate of a Midwestern university, with a rather typical small-town background. Pretty and bright, Pam had always dated boys, and in college she had been pinned to a fraternity man.

"I liked him well enough," she said, "but when the other girls would talk about the way they felt toward their boy friends, I had to admit to myself that I didn't feel that way at all. I never had—toward anyone. They'd describe kissing as an electric sensation, and tell how wonderful it made them feel, and I'd remember how I'd always tried to keep the love-making down to a minimum, because I didn't get anything out of it. I decided I was one of those frigid women you're always reading about these days. Then, a year later in Chicago, I met Helen, and for the first time in my life I knew there was good red blood in my veins."

From the beginning as roommates, Helen and Pam agreed that they would be "discreet" lovers. While Helen, who was never used to regular dates with men, does not now date them as often as Pam does, three or four times a month she has dinner or drinks with one. Twice a month the girls entertain a mixed crowd of their mutual friends, and very often they attend dinner parties and informal get-togethers to which these friends invite them. When I was a college senior Pam was a freshman pledge in the sorority to which I belonged, and after she was graduated and working in Chicago we met again. At the time I was contemplating writing this book; if it hadn't been for that, our conversation would probably never have turned to the subject of homosexuality, and I might never have known that Pam's roommate was more than a roommate to her.

"None of our friends suspect," she said. "We go out of our way to give the impression that we're no more close than any two women sharing an apartment, and perhaps less close. We never call one another by affectionate names around people. Neither of us have ever been to a homosexual night club, nor have we any other homosexual friends. We abhor that sort of thing. We just need each other—and normal friends. This way it's not like being exiles or misfits in the world."

I asked Pam if Helen ever became jealous of the men Pam perpetually dates, if they ever quarreled over them.

She said, "Sometimes we have silly fights about it, but they don't last long. Helen knows I don't like men physically. She knows I kiss them good night sometimes, and I hate it. Yet she knows I have to go out on dates or I don't feel right. We have a good understanding. We're sure of each other. And the most important part of our relationship is that we both feel the same way about homosexuality. We're homosexuals, and I guess when we're together we're glad of it, but on the other hand, we're not *proud* of it. We wouldn't want anyone to know."

Dates, in Pam's life, are ammunition with which to answer the inner voice that whispers accusations she would rather not hear. Instead of romance, these young men offer Pam a defense. She knows she is a lesbian; yet a large part of the Pam of today is made up of the Pam of yesterday, the high-school boys' sweetheart, the fraternity man's queen. While she can be one or the other, and her nature has made her choose lesbianism, she must still live with both Pams.

Today's Pam says, "I love Helen."

And at the same time, yesterday's Pam says, "I have a date with a man every week end."

The two Pams don't seem to fight. They seem to exist side by side, one for sure and one for show—but both the same person.

Many lesbians who live as roommates and practice discretion are less well adjusted inwardly than Pam and Helen. The voices of their consciences not only whisper, but shout. Two friends of mine who live under much the same circumstances as Pam and her roommate habitually worry over the possibility that their dates suspect their relationship. Carrie, the more aggressive and outspoken half of the pair, claims that Eleanor, her girl friend, is far too demonstrative before other people. Eleanor calls Carrie "darling," "lamb," and "sweetie," which would probably not be at all suspicious except for the fact that these utterances, when made in public, send Carrie into a tempestuous rage. Afterward she is usually sullen and cold to Eleanor, or she has already disappeared; gone back to their home alone to sulk.

"You simply have no discretion whatsoever," I heard Carrie accuse Eleanor one evening. "You give us away at the drop of a hat!"

Carrie has no awareness that it is she that gives them away.

One evening Carrie invited a man to have a drink in the apartment with her before they went out. As she mixed the cocktails, he looked through the various books on the bookshelf. Coming across one called "*Things as They Are*," by Gertrude Stein, he remarked casually, "This is Stein's book about lesbians, isn't it?"

Flustered, Carrie answered, "I don't know. It's not mine."

"But it is," her date protested. "There's an inscription in the front: 'To Carrie with my love always—E.'"

Carrie screamed at the shocked young man, "Well, are you satisfied now that you've snooped through everything in the house?"

Up until then, the young man had had no inkling of the true nature of Carrie's and Eleanor's relationship. On the few occasions when he saw Carrie after that time, his conversation revolved around the subject of psychoanalysis.

"It's helped a lot of folks," he told Carrie on their last date, "and there's no reason why it can't help you too, if you have a particular problem."

A similar incident occurred one week end when Carrie went to Long Island to visit friends and sail on the Sound. Eleanor did not accompany her, but expected to see her when Carrie returned, late that evening. A bad storm arose, and Carrie's friends suggested she stay overnight, which Carrie agreed to do. Eleanor, meanwhile, having heard the weather reports, was frantic for fear something had happened to the boat. Toward dawn, when there was still no sign of Carrie, Eleanor was beside herself. At seven in the morning, after a sleepless night, she called Carrie's friends, awakening them, and consequently launching Carrie into another of her fits of anger.

"You don't have to act so indignant!" Eleanor said. "It would never have happened if you'd thought to call and say you were spending the night."

Carrie retorted bitterly, "Do you suppose I want them to think we're so damn attached to each other that I have to check in and out with you all the time? Now," she added testily, "you've made a complete fool of me!"

Carrie's fierce obsession with "discretion" destroys the very impression that she strives to give. Her irrational behavior over things that might very well happen between any two roommates makes Carrie's and Eleanor's friends wonder if they really are typical career women sharing the same apartment, or if perhaps there is something different about them and their living arrangement

The very word "discretion" implies that something is held in reserve; something is checked. If that something is one's true nature, it is often impossible to withhold its many facets, to predict its spontaneous outbursts, and to control its compulsions. Yet there are some—there are probably many—homosexuals who have learned to employ discretion and have it work well for them.

9.   LOVE THAT DARES NOT TELL ITS NAME

"All a lesbian really needs," I once heard a man declare, "is a good man! One who knows how to make love to a woman!"

In direct opposition, another told me, "Once a woman gets used to lesbian love-making, she never wants any other kind. It's like a drug."

Both men make the mistake of assuming that sexual technique is the all-important consideration in heterosexual and homosexual relationships. On the one hand it is believed that the male who learns to be a skilled manipulator of the female body can bring joy to any woman, even a lesbian. The female body in essence becomes a parade ground on which the male drills, and sensuality becomes a science. On the other hand it is believed that when a lesbian makes love, she practices some form of sexual black magic irresistible to her partner, and unavailable to the male.

To many people today, technique is the tin god of modern sexuality, and "doing what comes naturally" merely a phrase from a song everyone was humming in the forties. The simple pleasure of "petting" has been translated into the complex problem of "foreplay." Love is a course, and sexual intercourse is the final examination.

Many of my heterosexual friends who talk in terms of technique emphasize the role the clitoris plays in homosexual eroticism. They assume, and rightly so, I believe, that the majority of female homosexuals rely for the most part on the sensations produced by the manipulations of the clitoris during sexual congress. In Kinsey's study of females who had homosexual experiences, this assumption is borne out, just as it is in the more recent study *Sex Variants*, by Dr. Henry.

"If you agree with me that the lesbian is mainly a clitoridean type of woman," a friend of mine argued, "then you have to agree also that the lesbian has the advantage over the male in making love to a woman. She's touching a familiar body. Her technique's bound to be better!"

This argument, like many with respect to the nature of the lesbian's sexual experience, concentrates solely on the nature of the lesbian's sexual experience, concentrates solely on the physical, and ignores the more important psychological factors involved in homosexuality. Those who worship at the altar of technique perhaps overlook the fact that if the psyche is unwilling, no amount of technique can persuade it; and if the psyche is willing, no lack of technique can dissuade it. While a heterosexual may experience homosexual intercourse, and vice versa, the technique employed is probably the least consideration in determining the extent to which either experiment will continue. A much more important consideration is the psychological receptivity. With regard to the lesbian in particular, the gratification she will ultimately enjoy and desire to re-experience in her homosexual relations is directly related to this psyche of hers, whose roots are deep in her past. As Dr. Frank Caprio stated in his study *Female Homosexuality*, "Today, psychiatrists know that sexual inversion is an emotional aberration—a disorder of psychological rather than genetic origin and therefore should be treated by psychological methods."

What, then, is the nature of the female homosexual's "emotional aberration"? What is it she looks for in the love act, and finds only in the arms of another woman?

As we have already noted, homosexuality is regarded by the majority of psychiatrists and psychologists as an arrest in development, both mental and physical. The female who cannot graduate from clitoridean sensuality to vaginal sensuality is often the same girl who cannot pass from love of her own sex to that of the opposite sex. She may then remain frigid, or search for satisfaction in a lesbian relationship. Freud believed that in the course of the homosexual's development, her personality remained fixed at a point somewhere between auto-erotism (self-love) and object love (love of another person). Therefore, he concluded, she cannot do without physical features similar to her own in her sexual partner.

"A man is another person," Nora, the lesbian in Djuna Barnes's novel *Nightwood* complains, "a woman is yourself . . . on her mouth you kiss your own. If she is taken you cry that you have been robbed of yourself."

Here we have a typical homosexual's argument for the familiar, as opposed to the unfamiliar. The lesbian looks for herself in her lover, and finds her own femininity revealed to her by another feminine body. Simone de Beauvoir, in her discussion of the lesbian in *The Second Sex*, states that many women turn to homosexuality to cultivate the treasures of their femininity. When a woman caresses her own body, Beauvoir writes, she still does not know how her breasts seem to a strange hand, or how her body is felt to react under a strange hand. A man can reveal to a woman the existence of her flesh as she herself perceives it, but not what it is to others.

"It is only when her fingers trace the body of a woman whose fingers in turn trace her body," she states, "that the miracle of the mirror is accomplished."

The narcissistic enjoyment many lesbians receive from their intimacies may well spring from a desire on the part of the homosexual woman to "cultivate the treasures of femininity," just as Simone de Beauvoir states. In an article entitled

"Men, Women and Dresse," in the magazine *Psychoanalysis* (Winter 1953), Dr. Theodore Reik theorizes that women, unlike men, pay particular attention to their physical charms in order to compensate for an original sexual inferiority feeling. He cites a remark reported by the well-known pediatrician Dr. Benjamin Spock concerning a little girl's observations when she saw a nude boy.

"But he's so fancy," she complained to her mother, "and I'm so plain."

Girls, Reik believes, overcome the "handicap" of their lack of a penis by becoming proud of their figures and of the other gifts nature bestows upon them as they grow older. Their vanity, which develops side by side with their figure, "is still a reaction to the unconscious feelings of being put at a disadvantage." The homosexual, who cannot emotionally accept the role of a woman, perhaps demands double compensation. It is not enough for her to be proud of her femininity, for she is perpetually unsure of it, and unwilling to accept a subordinate position to the male. Thus, not only does she refuse the male, but she realizes herself twofold with another female.

While the lesbian may be said to be fleeing "to herself" in the homosexual embrace, what she believes she is fleeing *from* is also a large consideration in determining the nature of her "emotional aberration." Many lesbians with whom I have discussed the differences between the sexual attitude in lesbian intercourse and the feelings they have experienced in their few flights into the world of heterosexuality dwell on the basic emotional differences of the sexes.

"With a woman," one friend told me, "I can relax and enjoy closeness, nearness—the physical luxury of simply lingering in the arms of someone who *enjoys* caressing my body, as much as I do hers. Women don't have to prove anything by their love when they're together. A man, when he is with a woman, must prove his virility. And another thing—I don't feel deserted by a woman when our love-making is finished. I feel all the more a part of her. With men, it's different. You have neither the leisure beforehand nor the security after. Men leave you lonely even when they stay beside you."

The female's fear that she is (a) a proving ground and (b) an object to be discarded after the act of intercourse can sometimes serve to send her along other paths in search of sexual satisfaction. Again in the magazine *Psychoanalysis* (Summer 1953) Theodore Reik discusses "The Emotional Differences of the Sexes." Every analyst who has treated many women, Reik writes, is familiar with the female's fear of desertion. Men rarely feel this fear. "It really seems as if the masculine saying 'Love them and leave them' has a pendant, a counterpart, in a feminine warning, 'Don't love them or they will leave you' . . . The male," Reik continues, "who has shown such an immediacy, urgency, and intensity of sexual desire, has very soon after the emission the wish to leave the body of the woman."

Reik, as well as Freud, Marie Bonaparte, and Helene Deutsch, among others, have stressed the "masochistic" nature of the normal female, whose acceptance of "injuries" or "slights" is indispensable to her acceptance of the whole of her sexuality. The lesbian, whose psychological maladjustment renders her doubly vulnerable to any masculine hurt, cannot accept this passive, submissive role. To her it is abuse, and from it she flees to homosexual "protection."

The male's urgency in the sex act is often interpreted by the lesbian as a lack of tenderness, inconsiderateness, and brutality. She who does not desire to be conquered by the male, or possessed by him, criticizes that very proclivity in him for aggressiveness and physical domination which the normal female submits to gratefully and lovingly. Because the lesbian fears penetration by the male, and subsequently resents it and abhors it, she may commonly complain that the male wants the female only as a sexual object, and not also as a love object and a friend.

Needless to point out, there are many instances where a woman who has turned from heterosexuality to homosexuality, or who has remained fixed at the homosexual level throughout her experience, actually did experience a lack of tenderness, inconsiderateness, and brutality at the hands of a man. Not all of the lesbian's opinions with regard to homosexuality are seen through the spectacle of her neuroses.

In Dr. Caprio's study *Female Homosexuality*, he has this to say with regard to "psychic traumas":

"It is not too difficult to understand how a young girl who during her puberty years is sexually accosted by her father or brother, an uncle or some elderly man, may develop an aversion to men and sex. I have encountered a good many lesbians who gave a history of some unpleasant sexual experience in adolescence."

Further, he states: "Many men are responsible for women turning against sex in general. The use of obscene language, selfishness, brutality, or a lack of adequate technique all tend to traumatize the normal sexual feelings of a woman."

As a rule, however, the woman inclined toward normal sexuality does not suddenly become a lesbian simply because she has been ill treated by a man. One factor alone can never suffice to explain the lesbian's character, any more than a single bad experience can suffice to cause lesbianism in a woman. While many lesbians swear that they became homosexual because the male was a brute at some point in their development, this explanation cannot always be accepted as a logical one. Dr. Caprio puts is this way: "In some cases, however, the lesbian is merely looking for an excuse to explain why she became homosexual. Not every girl who suffers a psychic trauma during childhood or adolescence became a lesbian. Much depends on the individual reaction to the particular traumatic experience."

In the small town where I was born and raised, an incidence of homosexuality caused great furor on the part of the townspeople. At the time I was only eleven, and all I knew about the gossip being circulated was the fact that the husky, athletic woman who ran a riding academy outside the city and the wife of a prominent businessman, as well as mother to his two children, had gone off somewhere together. I remember hearing masked references to the scandal as my parents and our neighbors discussed it in the living room, while I listened outside on the porch.

"Why, Ginny was no more strange than you or I," my mother remarked to the lady next door, "and she's had two children. It's impossible."

"She and that Powers woman were always together. When Tom was away on trips, the Powers woman would stay over," our neighbor answered, "but I never thought anything like that was in the wind."

My father said, "Tom was too much of a businessman, and he drank too much. He had a foul temper. Everyone knew he gave her a good crack now and then, but she never seemed to mind. She was so docile. . . . No, Tom didn't give her much love, but why did she have to resort to *that* for it!"

"Why, indeed!" everyone chorused.

As I grew older I found out more about this woman who left her home and her family to run off with a lesbian. A quiet, shy young woman, she had grown up motherless in a household of two older brothers and a strict, mean-tempered father. Her main interest in life was riding, and most of her spare time was spent out at the stables. She was the last one in her high-school class to marry, and hers was a "practical" marriage. Husband and wife had known each other all their lives. He was a friend of her brothers, and much like her father in disposition. Neither were particularly sociable or popular. After their marriage, she continued to ride daily. A nurse attended their children, and a maid did the housework. Her husband was a very successful businessman, a somewhat aloof person who traveled constantly and drank himself to sleep in an effort to fight off his chronic insomnia.

When the riding academy changed hands and the Powers woman came from Cleveland to head it, the two women became fast friends. The husband enjoyed Miss Powers too, and the threesome seemed to get along very well. Then one evening Tom Powers returned unexpectedly from a business trip and discovered the pair on the couch in the living room, disrobed and making love. Irately he ordered them both from the house, hitting his wife on the jaw and causing a fracture. A few days later, his wife and Miss Powers left town together.

One can only speculate as to why this woman, who was a wife and a mother, became a homosexual. Possibly she found in this older woman the mother she had never had, and who would offer her the tenderness she yearned for after years of mental suffering under a sharp-tempered father and then under a husband of similar temperament. Perhaps because she had never known a real mother, she could not be one to her own children, whose care was left to a nursemaid. Perhaps she realized in Miss Powers a feeling of "belonging," which is part of love, and which she could not realize with her husband, whom she had not loved. And perhaps after years of being withdrawn and introverted, when she found another human being whose love was companionate as well as passionate, she surrendered everything she had to it.

Another frequent motive for homosexuality, already described in Chapter 2, is a desire to play a masculine role. In such cases the sexual act is a homosexual imitation of hetero-sexual congress. Dr. Henry in his study *Sex Variants* cited several descriptions of this situation.

"In my relationship with these women I pretended I was a man," one said, "and that I had a penis which penetrated the other woman. . . . We talked about having babies and giving a woman a baby. . . ."

"If I'm going with a woman and she touches my breasts," another very masculine lesbian said, "I don't want to have anything else to do with her. . . . Just let a woman touch my breasts and it drives my passion away." This same lesbian spoke of her clitoris as though it were a penis, bragging that is was two inches long, had erections, and "some women think I have an emission."

The desire on the part of these masculine lesbians to penetrate their partners, or their partners' desire to be penetrated by them, is sometimes satisfied with the use of penis substitutes. Such instruments are as old as antiquity, though probably not used too frequently by many female homosexuals today. Johann Jakob, in his study *Sexual Life in Ancient India*, describes a document that tells of lesbian practices in Indian harems, during which the women wore artificial penises. Dr. Caprio says that "an artificial rose-colored penis could be purchased by women in China without embarrassment," and reports that a Dr. Oscar Baumann discovered that among the Zanzibar women a carved, oiled, sickle-shaped piece of ebony was used.

Today such instruments are usually called "dildos" among lesbians. Dr. Henry reported a few evidences of their use in his case studies, and related a part of the history of a lesbian who described one such substitute:

"It was made out of a rubber hose and a condom was used over it. She painted it to look like a penis, the color of the skin. It took a genius to make it look as much like a man's organ as it did."

Dildos come in a variety of forms. Some may be held in the hand; others are worn by one partner or used in single or double form. It is my belief that they are not frequently employed in most relationships between two lesbians. In the first place, they are not generally available to most lesbians, and secondly, to many there is relatively little desire for actual penetration, the clitoris being the main organ for their gratification.

On the whole, I would say that most female homosexuals merely feel occasional melancholy awareness of their inability to possess a woman as a man. At such times, rather than attempt to find a substitute penis, I think they more often "lie there wishing perhaps to be a man for a moment," as Anaïs Nin describes it in "Winter of Artifice."

Whatever means the lesbian resorts to for the end result in her sexual satisfaction, it seems apparent that the psychological factors of her make-up outweigh any physiological factors. However great the lesbian's satisfaction is in homosexual intercourse, it depends ultimately more upon her emotional needs than upon her sexual needs.

10.   THE BISEXUAL

One way of explaining homosexuality is to assume that everyone has a bisexual make-up. Many scientists, psychiatrists, psychologists, and sociologists have attempted to prove that bisexuality exists in human beings both in the psychological and in the anatomical senses.

Biochemists discovered that the feminine and masculine products of the sex organs (estrogen and androgen) could be found in the urine of both sexes.

Freud explained that parts of the male sex apparatus are also to be found in the female, although in a rudimentary condition, and vice versa, "as though the individual were neither man nor woman, but both at the same time, only rather more than one the other."

Dr. Otto Weininger in his book *Sex and Character* refers to the polar elements of male and female sexuality in the same individual. He claims there exists in every human being male and female character elements.

And Dr. Wilhelm Stekel in his book *Bisexual Love* has this to say regarding the bisexual nature of mankind:

"There is no exception to this rule. Normal persons show distinct bisexual period up to the age of puberty. The heterosexual then represses his homosexuality."

Time and time again in psychoanalytic literature reference

is made man's and woman's predisposition to bisexuality. It is presumed by the majority of authorities that genetically all higher living beings are built on a bisexual basis, and that all carry within them the fundamentals of the other sex.

Under unfavorable conditions such as we have examined in past chapters, the homosexual component comes to the fore. In certain types the person who gives vent to his homosexual inclinations at the same time indulges his heterosexual ones. He is the bisexual, the person who consorts sexually with both sexes.

Today among homosexuals the word "bisexual" is more and more used and abused. To hear many homosexuals talk together, one would think there were no homosexuals left in the world, that all of us, in reality, were bisexuals. Peculiarly enough, in the eyes of society the bisexual seems less a freak than the homosexual. He or she who plays on both teams is often considered more acceptable than that person who limits himself exclusively to homosexual practices. Homosexuals realize this and frequently describe themselves as bisexual as a form of defense, even though they are not involved in any way with the opposite sex.

One evening at a gay party I heard this song:

Don't say I'm queer, dear,
Say I'm bisexual,
A latent heterosexual.
Say my inclinations are double-gaited,
My normality is just belated.
Say my personality has made me fated
To be bisexual or trisexual, intellectual, ineffectual,
But when you speak to me, please, my dear,
Make it clear,
Although I have a complex
About the same sex
I'm no queer.

Some homosexuals who have never had heterosexual relations more than once cling to the memory as their proof that they are not true homosexuals. Some who have carried on heterosexual relations for an appreciable period, but who have since passed over completely to homosexuality, state emphatically that they are bisexuals, because in their past there were heterosexual experiences.

Benjamin Karpman in his book *The Sexual Offender and His Offenses* states that these homosexuals are not what is meant when he refers to bisexuals, for they are merely homosexuals with a bisexual past.

"What we mean by a bisexual," he says, "is a man (or woman) who continues to live on both sides of the tracks; not one who once lived on one side and then moved over to the other."

Using Karpman's definition of the bisexual, let us speculate now as to the reason for a woman consistently to switch from the same sex to the opposite sex and back again. Karpman himself pondered this question and decided that the bisexual woman is often a homosexual who simulates heterosexuality to escape the stigma of spinsterhood and enjoy greater material comfort by marrying.

This opinion is partially supported by Dr. George Henry's findings in his study of seventeen bisexual women, eleven of whom married. The following are comments concerning six of the eleven's reasons for marriage:

"My sole desire was to escape the tyranny of my mother, so at twenty I married the man I was engaged to, a wealthy Jew four years older than I was. . . ."

". . . After several months of absolute indifference on the part of the singer (a woman) I decided to marry this month. He was a sympathetic individual, understood my interest in women, and it seemed that we might establish a pleasant household. . . ."

"By this time I had my mother on my hands and nothing for our maintenance. I welcomed any aid and for the sake of security I married a sixty-four-year-old widower who was very kind to me."

"When I was twenty-two I married a large handsome man. He was imposing in appearance but actually he was boastful, empty, and little more than a shell. It seemed to be a way out. . . ."

"When I was eighteen I got married to him in order to help Mother. . . ."

"Finally when I was twenty I married him. I don't know why I did. I had no pleasure during courtship and had no interest in men."

Three of the eleven married bisexuals had married because they were already pregnant. Only two actually seemed to desire marriage for marriage's sake.

It is probably quite a valid argument that many bisexual women are actually homosexuals "covering up." This argument, however, perhaps does not take into account a goodly number of bisexual women who need both sexes, not for material gain or to escape the stigma of spinsterhood, but for deeper, less obvious psychological reasons.

"I think I get more violent physical reactions from a man and more mental from a woman," another of Henry's bisexual case states. "I would rather be with a woman even though I get more thrill from a man. . . . I have sex dreams all the time and I'm always with men. Once or twice I had pleasant dreams that I was with women. . . ."

Here is evidenced the inconsistent yearnings of a bisexual type who cannot decide which sex she prefers. Not infrequently among the bisexuals I have encountered, this indecision is often responsible for an inability truly to enjoy relations with either sex. Tanja, a very attractive little Russian girl whom I know, is perpetually running from men to women and then back again.

"At a party," she told me once, "if I attend with a woman, I want always to make love with a man there. Still, if it is the other way around, and I attend with a man, then I want to make love with a woman there. I don't which I want, but when I am with one I want the other, and vice versa. It is a great dilemma!"

Perhaps one reason a woman may desire both a man and another woman is explained in my friend Judy's response to my question: "Why both sexes?" Judy is married and extremely devoted to her young husband, as he is to her. While they enjoy sexual relations, Judy claims that her husband's sexual needs are different from hers at times.

"Sometimes," she said, "I want a man to take me, to conquer me, to be the master. Other times I just want to relax and be cuddled and pampered. He doesn't understand that. Sex for him is an act to be started and finished, with a beginning and an end. To me, now and then, it is just a relaxation without any beginning or end—just a pleasant interlude of pleasant sensations. For that you need a woman."

This attitude was expressed by Pearl M., another of Henry's bisexual cases. She said, "Sexual relations with my husband were more satisfying than those with Pamela, but this is so effortless. . . . As one grows older every sexual relationship, especially with a man, is an effort."

In *Women's Barracks*, by Tereska Torres, a woman who claims to enjoy both sexes states that with men there is a need rarely satisfied, "a need for simple caressing."

"This was love between women," Miss Torres writes, "to be able to rest their heads together, to hold hands. The stroking of a knee, the kissing of a shoulder—all this was part of love between two women, and this in itself could suffice."

The bisexual woman then may be said sometimes to be torn between a desire for complete submission to the male on the one hand and casual, leisurely caressing with a female on the other. At least this is one type of bisexual woman, differing from the type that uses heterosexuality for material or social gain.

Still another type, distinguished from these two by her own unawareness of the reasons for her bisexuality, is the nymphomaniac bisexual who frantically consorts with both sexes at a fierce and frenzied pace.

"Geegee isn't homosexual," I heard a man remark once about a woman acquaintance of ours who was having an affair with another woman. "She just likes sex—any kind of sex. She's just insatiable. There aren't enough men to go around."

And Geegee herself had this to say: "I don't care what sex the person is as long as it's sex."

A closer look at Geegee might disprove her and our friend's theory that she is oversexed. While any attempt on my part to delve into the psychological make-up of Geegee would be crudely amateurish, there are some significant aspects of her personality that might give insight into Geegee even to the most unschooled layman. Geegee's entire interest in life is concerned with sex. Her reading matter, her conversation, her jokes, her interest in people, and her physical energies are concentrated wholly upon anything and everything pertaining to sexuality. Yet Geegee herself is the first to admit that she has to be "good and crocked" (drunk) to bring herself to have relations with anyone. A steady drinker, bordering on the alcoholic, Geegee usually is good and crocked, and usually does manage to have at least one affair of some kind per day. Not a whore, she is as indiscriminate as a whore, and unnaturally proud of her notoriety as a "nymph." Perhaps the biggest clue concerning Geegee was given in a remark made by her ex-husband. "It's funny that sex is all she thinks about," he said, "and yet she never stays sober to enjoy it. She doesn't even know what's happening when she's physically involved. Once I told her I thought her whole trouble was that she was under-sexed, and she almost killed me for saying that. She called me every name in the book and told me to get out of her sight, and after I left our apartment, while I was waiting for the elevator, I could hear her inside, still throwing books at the door I'd slammed behind me."

Probably many of the nymphomaniac bisexuals are like Geegee, searching for any reassurance that they are not frigid, unattractive, or asexual. Unable to feel such assurance in their own hearts, they break these same hearts over and over by running the never ending rat race of erotomania.

If the bisexual woman is something of an enigma, the man who is attracted to her is even more puzzling. Of those men I have known who were attracted to bisexuals, I have observed five types. One is the man completely unaware of the woman's dual nature. Another is the man who is aware of her duality, but who refuses to believe that the homosexual side is "anything serious." Clyde, a man of this type, once remarked to me about his fiancée, "Oh, I know she has that *thing* about women, but it's just a hangover from her boarding-school days. It doesn't bother me in the least." Refusing to consider a lesbian as a rival, he blithely pretends the whole neurosis doesn't amount to anything.

Charlotte N., another of Dr. Henry's bisexual cases, married but in love with a woman, has this to say concerning her husband's feelings in the matter:

"My husband is masculine but he's happy-go-lucky. He doesn't seem to take things seriously. He feels it is just a lark and that I will get over it in time. . . . If I could be sure that this girl would remain faithful I would be willing to end my marriage. . . ."

A third type of man who is attracted to the bisexual woman is the one who is thoroughly aware of her condition and morosely unhappy over it. Still, he continues to love her, hoping against hope that he can cure her. Perhaps there is some significance in the fact that he clings to his unhappy situation so desperately, coddling the calamity as though it were his good fortune instead of his misfortune.

"I knew how Billie felt about women when I married her," one such man told me once, "but I was determined not to let it spoil my love for her. She's put me through a hell on earth, but it doesn't matter. . . . Nothing matters except that I have her with me."

Perpetually consulting psychologists, psychiatrists, and therapists, this husband is never satisfied with any answers he can elicit from his inner self concerning his disheartening marital situation. A true sufferer, ostensibly, he seems to thrive on his peculiar form of unhappiness. "She's worth it!" he always declares adamantly, and then adds with the air of one anticipating an injury, "Don't you think so?"

A fourth type is the man who enjoys his woman's homosexual proclivities, sometimes to the point of encouraging them in her. Of the men of this kind that I have met none was bisexual himself. In each case, the man's interest lay in urging on a lesbian relationship between the woman he loved and another woman. Whatever his vicarious pleasure may be termed by a doctor, I think it is fairly obvious that this kind of man in some way identifies himself with the woman he loves, and either vicariously or actually seduces the woman *she* loves.

The last type of many whom I have observed drawn to the bisexual female is the bisexual male. This is not to say that a homosexual male and a lesbian team up together, for in such instances there is rarely any physical attraction, but merely a fraternal feeling. Two bisexuals, however, sometimes mate, and enjoy relations with each other, while at the same time each enjoys relations with the same sex. Of the two such marriages I know of, both seem relatively well-adjusted unions.

"We get along splendidly," one of the wives commented once, "because we love each other, and we know that no matter how many times we leave each other for a homosexual involvement, we haven't really left each other. We belong together—people, time, or place won't change that."

"And the women in your life?" I asked. "How do they take to their marriage?"

"They are jealous, naturally," she answered, "but in a way, behind it all, I sometimes think they're relieved, too."

"Relieved?"

She said, "Yes, because they know that I'm ambivalent, and they know Peter, my husband. They would rather know I'm with him than picture me running wildly from man to man the way some bisexuals do. In Peter, they know, I have a home, and they know too that they are welcome in that home—that Peter understands."

The true bisexual probably has a more difficult time adjusting than does the homosexual. As Karpman put it in his summary of the bisexual in *The Sexual Offender and His Offenses*:

"The bisexual, knowing that his heterosexuality is socially approved while his homosexuality is socially condemned, is in many cases the subject of greater conflict. If he is predominantly homosexual by inclination, he will nevertheless make a strong attempt to maintain his heterosexuality for social reasons. If he is predominately heterosexual by inclination, he will experience all the more conflict because of his occasional lapses into homosexuality."

"What if you were shipwrecked on an island?" a lesbian asked a bisexual female at a party one evening. "Which sex would you want to be shipwrecked with you? Suppose you had to choose. Wouldn't you choose a woman?"

"Yes," her friend answered, "I would choose a woman— because nine times out of ten, it would be a man who would come to rescue us."

11.   UNCONSCIOUS HOMOSEXUALITY

The words of the old adage "It is better to mate than to sublimate" might well be reversed in the mind of the unconscious homosexual to read: "It is better to sublimate than to mate."

By psychological definition, sublimation is the process of deflecting sexual aims to interests of a nonsexual and socially approved nature. While this sounds like a rare feat for human nature to perform, it is not an uncommon one. We are all familiar with the unmarried adult who is still "waiting for Mr. Right to come along." In many cases even well beyond middle age, such individuals murmur remorsefully that as yet Mr. Right (or Miss Right) has failed to show up, and there is nothing left to do but to continue living in the lonely cocoon of bachelorhood or spinsterhood. This is not to say that all people who have never married are unconscious homosexuals, or that all those who are unconscious homosexuals have experienced any conscious desire for a homosexual relationship. It is simply to point out, as Robert Caprio did in his study of lesbianism, that there are many people who have never felt any sexual attraction to the opposite sex, but who have been too repressed to give way to any physical manifestations of love for members of the same sex.

Fritz Wittels, in his essay "Homosexuality" published in

Elements of Psychoanalysis, includes in this camp such eccentrics as misers, collectors, bookworms, and fanatic lovers and protectors of animals who prefer pets to men, because animals are no danger to them. As the alternative to homosexual panic, Wittels concludes, this type of unconscious homosexual chooses narcissism because it promises him peace.

Some of these individuals may resort to masturbation as a sexual outlet; others may exhaust their energies in their careers. In Freud's study of Leonardo da Vinci, he concluded that Da Vinci was an unconscious homosexual who sublimated his sex drive into a frantic preoccupation with his varied professions, so that ultimately he was too busy to think about sex. The career woman who puts all of her workday and leisure energies into her job might well be of similar bent.

Many times unconscious homosexuals are able to sublimate by choosing careers that allow them to give vent to their hidden homosexual aggression. Dr. George Sprague, writing on the "Varieties of Homosexual Manifestations" in *The Homosexuals*, discussed this in terms of the male homosexual. He said, "He may so modify the expression as to make it socially acceptable through the process of sublimation. In this case we see certain forms of interest and activity which have a symbolic or displaced homosexual value, as in the case of the designer of clothing, the teacher in a boy's school, or the professional boxer. . . ."

Edmund Bergler, in his book *Fashion and the Unconscious*, theorized that these sublimated homosexual inclinations on the part of many male dress designers are responsible for such uncomfortable styles as the hobble skirt, which made it practically impossible for the woman wearing one to walk, and such unattractive styles as "the flat look," which defeminizes the female.

In a song of several years back, "Anatole of Paris," made popular by Danny Kaye, a male hat designer tells of the insane creations he dreams up for his female clientele. At the end of the song he squeals, "Why do I do it? Because—I hate women!"

Not all unconscious homosexuals are able to sublimate successfully, and they therefore build up various neurotic defense reactions to situations that call to mind their abnormal leanings. In discussing this, Caprio mentions specifically the man who will assault or even kill a man who makes improper advances to him. Not all reactions of unconscious homosexuals to homosexual situations are this drastic, of course, but all are likely to be violent.

Caprio believes that women, more often than men, are susceptible to the type of mental breakdown brought on by unconscious homosexual cravings. Because they usually have very little knowledge of homosexuality, he thinks, and because they are usually too inhibited to seek the help of a psychiatrist, they are more vulnerable. He tells of one case where the female patient had auditory hallucinations during which she heard voices say to her that she was a pervert, and that she wanted unnatural relations with a woman friend she had known for many years. Another case he cited was that of an attractive woman in her early thirties, separated from her husband, who insisted that people on the street looked at her as if she were a lesbian. She went so far as to call upon the FBI and demand that they investigate the matter.

One way in which the unconscious homosexual defends himself or herself is in extreme promiscuity with the opposite sex. Wittels, in his essay, speaks of the Don Juan type of male, who seems to be sexually insatiable, confining his relations exclusively to women, one after the other. He would probably be the first to shout, "Queer!" at a suspected homosexual, and the last to admit that there is something a little queer about a man who cannot feel within himself the completeness and certainty of his own sex, and must constantly prove himself by running from one girl to the next to the next, ad infinitum.

His feminine counterpart, the aggressive "oversexed" woman, who literally seduces every man she can, betrays her identification with men by her desire for conquests, and exposes her uncertainties with regard to her sexuality.

Wittels mentions another defense for the unconscious homosexual—that of cruelty, or compulsive destructiveness. Men, he claimed, fearing an inner feminine drive, and wanting to give concrete evidence of their masculinity, often offer as proof their capacity for destruction, aggression, and even out-and-out sadism. By the same token, women who hate their femininity may develop sadistic natures as a way of saying that they are just as tough as men—and tougher! From there, Wittels believes, the road leads to the theory of the superman. During World War II, Germany produced its share of neurotics that might well fall into this category, in the figures of the Gestapo sadists and the lady who made lampshades out of human skin.

Alcohol also offers a flight from the fear of homosexuality. Many of the excessive and habitual drinkers in our midst are suffering from their suppressions of homosexual desires. Caprio, Karpman, Wittels, and Stekel, to name a few doctors who have studied the homosexual, believe that alcohol either (a) gives the repressed homosexual courage to indulge in homosexual phantasies, sometimes to the point of overt action, or (b) incapacitates him so that he eventually becomes stupefied and exchanges the dreaded homosexual component for narcissistic loneliness. In Charles Jackson's *The Lost Weekend*, the alcoholic hero was a repressed homosexual whose memories of homosexual adventures and desires returned to him during his periods of intoxication.

Obsessive jealousy in not infrequently rooted in unconscious homosexuality. Benjamin Karpman reports the story of a physician's wife who was obsessed with jealousy of her husband's female patients. She watched them through a secret peephole, in order to convince herself that there was nothing illicit going on. Unconsciously, Karpman explains, her interest was centered on the women, and not on her husband. Her excessive jealousy was no more than a mask for latent homosexuality.

Many times the way in which a man or woman prefers to perform sexual relations with the opposite sex is an index to unconscious homosexual cravings. Karpman mentions in this category women who like to have men perform cunnilingus on them, and who also like to perform fellatio on their husbands. The same, he states, is true of men who prefer such things as anal intercourse with their wives, as well as wanting fellatio practiced on them, or desiring to perform cunnilingus on the woman. He described the case of a married man, father of three children, who was never involved in any situation even remotely homosexual, and whose whole sexual life was devoted to heterosexuality. Nevertheless, there was one peculiarity about him. In marital relations he always wanted to be in the feminine position, and to have his wife in the masculine position. Also he enjoyed having his wife massage his breasts. While this man would be deeply insulted if he were told that he had a strong homosexual component, Karpman says, his behavior is a clear indication of its existence. Regular and consistent sexual practices that are inconsistent with a true heterosexual aim often are clues to an unconscious homosexual disposition.

"Paranoid" is a word being used more and more in society today. The person suffering from paranoia is one who is obsessed with delusions that he is being persecuted. Few of us are ever free from occasional fears that someone is talking about us, that someone is thinking poorly of us, or that we might not be receiving the approval we so much desire from other people. The paranoid, however, has a perpetual fear that he turns into a positive opinion that the world is out to get him. As Stekel and Freud and others pointed out, all paranoids are either conscious or unconscious homosexuals. The unconscious homosexual, who invariably has a paranoiac disposition, is, as Karpman puts it, using persecutory delusions to explain this fear he has of a homosexual attraction. Unable to admit that she desires a female, the unconscious homosexual woman makes herself believe that said female does not like her.

"'He hates me,'" Karpman writes, "is invariably a psychotic translation of 'I love him.'"

Another index of unconscious homosexual longings is the individual's feelings toward people of the same sex in social situations. "The club" is often mentioned in psychological literature as a particularly well-sublimated expression of homosexuality. Men who show a special preference for company of their own sex in clubs, men's fraternal organizations, gyms, and the armed forces are described as men who have much of this unconscious homosexuality in their make-up. Women too have their clubs and sororities, which are often likewise a means of successfully sublimating their unconscious homosexuality.

Karpman mentions the inability to undress or urinate in the presence of the same sex as often being an expression of underlying homosexual interest.

Unconscious homosexuality is sometimes found in the individual's choice of a heterosexual love. Women who are attracted to very feminine men are often sublimating their lesbian desires, just as is the passive man who chooses an aggressive, dominant woman. Karpman tells of one such man who, when praising his wife's body, said that she "looked for all the world like a young boy." George Sand, the very "virile" woman novelist, who dressed always as a man and smoked cigars, had a taste for young men and effeminate types. A busy heterosexual known to have had many affairs with males, and not actually known to have had any sexual relations with women, she made romantic history with her passionate love for the sickly, weak, and ethereal Chopin. Another type of heterosexual love that has an unconscious homosexual element to it is exemplified by the girl who marries a man because unconsciously she has fallen in love with his sister. To that category Karpman also adds the man who pursues a married woman because unconsciously he is attracted to her husband.

Impotence and frigidity are often conditioned on unconscious homosexuality. Analysts have discovered that the underlying factor is sometimes an early fixation on a parent or a sibling of the same sex. Again Benjamin Karpman cites a pertinent case. A man who suffers from periodic impotence finds that he can become potent again if he imagines that the thigh of the woman is really that of a middle-aged man or of a young boy. By rubbing his penis against the imagined male thigh, he is able to have an erection. The implications of his phantasy, Karpman states, he refuses to associate with any homosexual desire, preferring instead to remain willfully blind to his sexual situation.

"The opposite of love is not hate," Wilhelm Stekel once wrote. "It is indifference." If an individual suffers from unconscious homosexuality that he is unable to sublimate successfully or repress to the point where its intrusion is not manifest, he or she may find it difficult to be indifferent to members of the same sex. A neurosis may then develop which can be as slight as feeling discomfort at undressing before members of the same sex, or feeling antagonism toward obvious homosexuals, or feeling the need for homosexual phantasies during heterosexual love-making. On the other hand, the neurosis may grow to greater and more severe proportions that snowball into a sudden ugly climax, or an ultimate psychosis. All of us want to love and few of us know how, but some of us don't even know who or what. The unconscious homosexual whose neurosis is in fierce and full bloom plays a pitiful game of blind man's buff, the winner's prize of which, when revealed, repels and insults him.

12.　　　　　THERE'S A LAW AGAINST IT!

One of our national magazines runs a monthly column of cartoons depicting archaic laws that are still on the statute books, even though in modern times they are absurd as they are amusing. To the list of the law making holding hands in public illegal, the one punishing men who lift their forks at table before the women have picked up theirs, and the one forbidding a woman to use the telephone, we might well add another, just as absurd but not very amusing—the law against sodomy.

Webster's dictionary defines sodomy as "carnal copulation in any of certain unnatural ways," and while that is a definition that leaves much to the imagination, in that it is so vague it is a good definition. For sodomy can mean almost anything that might be construed as an unnatural sex act. Black's Law Dictionary describes it simply as a "crime against nature," and uses sodomy and buggery almost interchangeably.

Because in the United States laws concerning sex crimes are left to the jurisdiction of the individual states, for the most part, the thing that constitutes the criminal act of sodomy has many interpretations. Before beginning a discussion of the way in which the law pertains to lesbianism, let us examine briefly the legal attitudes toward sodomy in each of the forty-eight states. In each case the information was extracted from the state's statutes, and supplementary court interpretations of these.

ALABAMA employs the term "crime against nature" and states that the term sodomist includes "any person who commits a crime against nature, either with mankind or with any beast." Penetration must be proved; thus neither fellatio, cunnilingus, nor any likely lesbian practice is included. Penalty: two to ten years' imprisonment.

ARIZONA distinguishes sodomy from fellatio and cunnilingus. The former is "committed by the penetration of the mouth or rectum of any human being by the organ of any male person." The latter is any "willful . . . lewd or lascivious act upon or with the body of [or] any part or member thereof of any male or female person with the intent of arousing, appealing to or gratifying the lust or passion or sexual desires of either of such persons in any unnatural manner." Penalty for both: one to five years' imprisonment.

ARKANSAS punishes "sodomy or buggery" once there is proof of penetration. Penalty: five to twenty-one years.

CALIFORNIA employs the term "crime against nature" and states that it is a crime committed "with mankind or with animal" and "any sexual penetration, however slight, is sufficient to complete the crime." Any persons "participating in the act of copulating the mouth of one person with the sexual organ of another" are criminals. Fellatio and cunnilingus are clearly included under this law. Penalty: one to ten years for "sodomy"; not exceeding fifteen years for fellatio and cunnilingus.

COLORADO employs the term "crime against nature" and states that it includes "any unnatural carnal copulation committed . . . per anus or per os or in any way whatsoever." Penalty: one to fourteen years.

The solicitation of any unnatural copulation has a penalty of one month to two years in the county jail.

CONNECTICUT lists "bestiality and sodomy" as crimes and defines the offender as "any person who shall have carnal copulation with any beast, or who shall have carnal knowledge of any man, against the order of nature, unless forced or under fifteen years of age." Penalty: imprisonment for "not more than thirty years."

DELAWARE simply lists sodomy, describes it as "crime against nature," and provides that the offender ". . . shall be fined not exceeding one thousand dollars, and shall be imprisoned not exceeding three years."

FLORIDA employs the term "crime against nature" with mankind or beast, and adds that this "includes all acts of bestiality, and is not limited to the common law concept of sodomy." Penalty: imprisonment not exceeding twenty years.

GEORGIA defines sodomy as "carnal knowledge and connection against the order of nature, by man with man, or in the same unnatural manner with woman." Because penetration must be proved, "the crime of sodomy, in Georgia, cannot be committed between two women." Penalty: "Imprisonment at labor in the penitentiary for and during the natural life of the person convicted.

IDAHO employs the term "crime against nature" and states that it includes that committed with mankind or with animal, and "all unnatural copulations committed per os or per anus," and/or "any sexual penetration, however slight." Penalty: imprisonment for from one to five years.

ILLINOIS lists the crime as "sodomy, or other crime against nature," and disqualifies the offender from holding any office of trust thereafter, voting at any election, or serving as a juror "unless he or she is again restored to such rights by the terms of a pardon for the offense or otherwise according to law."

It was also ruled by the courts that the insertion of the tongue (cunnilingus) does not constitute the crime against nature.

It was also ruled in Illinois that husband and wife may commit the crime against nature.

INDIANA calls sodomy the "crime against nature," and adds, moreover, that "whoever entices, allures, instigates or aids any person under the age of twenty-one (21) years to commit masturbation or self-pollution shall be deemed guilt of sodomy." Also "the offense of copulation by the mouth" is included in this crime. Penalty: "fined not less than one hundred dollars ($100) nor more than one thousand dollars ($1000), to which may be added imprisonment in the state prison not less than two (2) years nor more than fourteen (14) years."

IOWA defines sodomy as any carnal copulation "in any opening of the body except sexual parts, with another human being or beast." Penalty: imprisonment for not more than ten years.

KANSAS states that the "crime against nature" with man or beast shall be deemed sodomy, and if proof of "actual lecherous penetration per os," is offered, that too is sodomy. Penalty: confinement and hard labor not exceeding ten years.

KENTUCKY has a statute against sodomy or "buggery" with man or beast, but does not define them. Penalty: two to five years.

LOUISIANA refers to the "crime against nature" and states that it is "unnatural carnal copulation by a human being with another of the same sex or the opposite sex or with an animal.

Emission is not necessary, and, when committed by a human being with another, the use of the genital organs of one of the offenders of whatever sex is sufficient to constitute the crime." Penalty: a fine of not more than two thousand dollars, or imprisonment for not more than five years, or both.

MAINE simply states that the "crime against nature, with mankind or with a beast, shall be punished by imprisonment for not less than one year, nor more than ten years."

MARYLAND clearly defines the sodomist as "every person who shall be convicted of taking into his or her mouth the sexual organ of any other person or animal, or who shall be convicted of placing his or her organ in the mouth of any person or animal, or who shall be convicted of committing any other unnatural or perverted sexual practice with any other person or animal." Upon conviction the sodomist "shall be fined not more than one thousand dollars ($1000.00) or be imprisoned . . . not exceeding ten years, or shall both be fined and imprisoned."

MASSACHUSETTS considers criminal sodomy and buggery, as well as "unnatural and lascivious acts." The former is punished with imprisonment for not more than twenty years, the latter with a fine "of not less than one hundred nor more than one thousand dollars or by imprisonment in the state prison for not more than five years or in jail or the house of correction for not more than two and one half years."

MICHIGAN calls sodomy "the abominable and detestable crime against nature either with mankind or with any animal," and states that emission need not be proved, but penetration, however slight, must be. Penalty: imprisonment for not more than fifteen years.

MINNESOTA defines the sodomist as "a person who carnally knows in any manner any animal or bird, or carnally knows any male or female person by the anus or by or with the mouth, or voluntarily submits to such carnal knowledge; or attempts sexual intercourse with a dead body," and such a person is subject to a penalty of imprisonment for not more than twenty years.

MISSISSIPPI considers "unnatural intercourse" the crime; yet an indictment charging a woman with having unnatural carnal intercourse by performing cunnilingus was not considered an offense of sodomy, since penetration is essential to the offense. Penalty: imprisonment for not more than ten years.

MISSOURI calls the crime "the abominable and detestable crime against nature . . . committed with mankind or with beast, with the sexual organs or the mouth." Penalty: imprisonment for not less than two years.

MONTANA refers to "the crime against nature" and mentions that penetration, however slight, is sufficient to prove the offense. Penalty: imprisonment for not less than five years.

NEBRASKA defines the sodomist as one who has "carnal copulation with a beast, or in any opening of the body except sexual parts with another human being." Penalty: imprisonment for not more than twenty years.

NEVADA's "crime against nature" is not further defined, but is penalized with a state prison term of not less than five years, "which many extend to life."

NEW HAMPSHIRE simply lists "offenses against chastity" and "lascivious acts" that are unnatural. Sodomy or buggery or the crime against nature is not mentioned. Penalty: imprisonment for not more than five years, or a fine of not more than one thousand dollars, or both.

NEW JERSEY considers sodomy, "or the infamous crime against nature, committed with man or beast," a high misdemeanor, punishable by a fine not exceeding one thousand dollars and/or imprisonment at hard labor for not more than twenty-one years.

NEW MEXICO does not define sodomy save to say it is committed with either man or beast, and penalizes the offender with imprisonment for not less than one year and/or a fine of not less than one thousand dollars.

NEW YORK has degrees of sodomy. Sodomy in the first degree involves intercourse by the anus, or by or with the mouth, without the consent of the other person, or when the other person is unable to give consent by reason of mental or physical weakness or immaturity, or when resistance is forcibly overcome, or when resistance is made impossible by fear of bodily harm, or when it is prevented by stupor, drugs, or alcohol, or when the other person is unconscious. Knowing any "animal or bird," or attempting sexual intercourse with a corpse, also is first-degree sodomy. Second-degree sodomy is a relationship with a person under the age of eighteen years, under conditions not amounting to first-degree sodomy. Third-degree sodomy is knowing a person, male or female, "by the anus or with the mouth under circumstances not amounting to sodomy in the first degree or sodomy in the second degree." Penalty varies, depending upon degree and circumstances.

NORTH CAROLINA includes in the "crime against nature" all kindred acts of a bestial character whereby "degraded and perverted sexual desires are sought to be gratified," and also unnatural intercourse between male and male. Penalty: imprisonment for from five to sixty years.

NORTH DAKOTA penalizes anyone who carnally knows any animal, or bird, or male or female person by the anus or with the mouth; anyone who voluntarily submits to such carnal knowledge: and anyone who attempts intercourse with a dead body. Penalty: imprisonment for not less than one year or more than ten years.

OHIO: In this state, "whoever has carnal copulation with a beast or in any opening of the body, except sexual parts, with another human being, shall be guilty of sodomy and shall be imprisoned in the penitentiary not more than twenty years." It is significant that in the court decision in the case of the State versus Forquer, it was ruled that the act of cunnilingus is not made a crime by the statutes of this state.

OKLAHOMA does not elaborate on the "detestable crime against nature, committed with mankind or with a beast," and penalizes this crime by imprisonment in the penitentiary for not more than ten years.

OREGON considers as a crime, along with sodomy, "any act of sexual perversity," either with mankind or with beast, or "sustained osculatory relations with the private parts of any man, woman or child," as well as the act of permitting such relations to occur "with his or her private parts." Penalty: one to fifteen years' imprisonment.

PENNSYLVANIA calls the sodomist "anyone who carnally knows in any manner any animal or bird, or carnally knows any male or female person by the anus or the mouth, or whoever voluntarily submits to such carnal knowledge." It is added that "carnal knowledge shall be deemed complete upon proof of penetration only." Penalty: a fine not exceeding five thousand dollars and/or imprisonment for not more than ten years.

RHODE ISLAND does not define "the abominable and detestable crime against nature," but punishes it by imprisonment for not more than twenty years or less than seven years.

SOUTH CAROLINA refers to "buggery" committed upon man or beast, and penalizes the offender with a fine of not less than five hundred dollars and/or imprisonment for five years.

SOUTH DAKOTA does not define the "crime against nature" beyond stating that "any sexual penetration, however slight, is sufficient to complete the crime." Penalty: imprisonment for not more than ten years.

TENNESSEE simply states that the "crime against nature," with mankind or with beast, is punishable by imprisonment in the penitentiary for not less than five or more than fifteen years.

TEXAS says sodomy is carnal copulation with a beast, or in any opening of the body of another human being except sexual parts, or use of the mouth on sexual parts of another human being for the purpose of having carnal copulation, or permission given by a person for these acts to be performed upon him or her. Penalty: two to fifteen years' imprisonment.

UTAH lists sodomy as the "crime against nature" committed with mankind or with any animal with either the sexual organs or the mouth. Penalty: three to twenty years' imprisonment.

VERMONT refers to "lewdness" as consisting of "a person participating in the act of copulating the mouth of one person with the sexual organ of another." Penalty: one to five years' imprisonment.

VIRGINIA speaks of the "crime against nature" as including any carnal knowledge of any brute animal, or male or female person, by the anus or with the mouth, or voluntarily submitting to such carnal knowledge, as well as intercourse with a corpse. Penalty: one to three years' imprisonment.

WASHINGTON defines the "crime against nature" exactly as Virginia does, and penalizes the offender by imprisonment for not more than ten years.

WEST VIRGINIA also defines the "crime against nature" in the same way as Virginia, excluding intercourse with a corpse. Penalty: imprisonment for not more than ten years.

WISCONSIN states that sodomy is a crime "which may be committed by the penetration of the mouth of any human being by the organ of any male person as well as by the penetration of the rectum." Penalty: one to five years' imprisonment.

WYOMING declares that the crime of sodomy can be committed "by having carnal knowledge of a man or beast." The sodomist is also one who "carnally knows any man or woman through the anus, or in any other manner contrary to nature; and whoever entices, allures, instigates or aids any person under the age of twenty-one (21) to commit masturbation or self-pollution." Penalty: five to twelve years' imprisonment.

In studying these statutes we come upon many quite incongruous facts, several of which pertaining to lesbianism I list here:

1. In the state of Georgia, sodomy cannot be committed between two women.

2. In the states of Illinois, Georgia, Mississippi, and Ohio, a man and wife or two males can be convicted of sodomy, but two lesbians performing the act of cunnilingus are not sodomists by law, nor are they guilty of any crime against nature.

3. In Alabama, Arkansas, Georgia, Michigan, Montana, Pennsylvania, South Dakota, and Wisconsin, there is no provision under the law for the "crime" of lesbian sexual intercourse, although there is for male homosexual and perverse heterosexual intercourse.

4. Only in Arizona and California is cunnilingus actually referred to in the statutes as an act constituting the crime of sodomy, although Minnesota makes it plain that carnal knowledge of any male or female person "by the anus or by or with the mouth" is sodomy.

5. In no instance is the word "homosexual" used, or the word "lesbian," in the statutes of any of the forty-eight states, yet the law pertains specifically to the sexual practices of members of the same sex. Neither is the word "homosexuality" employed at any time in these statutes.

It is clear that the legal codes have been much more lenient toward, or ignorant of, sexual relations between women than they have been toward sexual relations between men. This is borne out in practice as well as in theory. Dr. Kinsey, in his study of female sexual behavior, has this to say:

> Even in such a large city as New York, the records covering the years 1930 to 1939 show only one case of a woman convicted of homosexual sodomy, while

there were over 700 convictions of males on homosexual charges, and several thousand cases of males
prosecuted for public indecency, or for solicitation, or
for other activity which was homosexual. In our more
recent study of the enforcement of sex laws in New
York City we find three arrests of females on homosexual charges in the last ten years, but all of those
cases were dismissed, although there were some tens
of thousands of arrests and convictions of males
charged with homosexual activity in that same period
of time.

In Robert Caprio's study *Female Homosexuality* he states
that in his investigation of the matter in Washington, D.C., he
learned that no cases of female homosexuality that came to the
attention of the police were prosecuted. The usual practice, he
states, has been to dismiss the complaint and to regard the
incident as "misbehavior." The parties involved were merely
scolded. In sharp contrast, male inverts who are apprehended
by the police in the nation's capital are prosecuted in every
instance.

As an explanation for the differences in legal attitude
toward male homosexuality and female homosexuality, Kinsey
gave many varied reasons:

1. The fact that most people associate male homosexuality
with such acts as fellatio and rectal intercourse, which are
repugnant to them, whereas when they think of two lesbians
together, they visualize them as merely hugging and kissing,
and the whole situation seems somehow more emotional than
physical. Thus there is less righteous indignation over female
homosexuality.

2. The indiscretion of the male homosexual, which we
touched on the first chapter, Kinsey lists as a reason for the
public's concern about him.

3. Stemming from Biblical times, and evident in what Kinsey terms "the Catholic Code," is the idea of the sin in the waste of semen in all male activities that are non-coital; females, on the other hand, obviously cannot commit the same sin.

Robert Caprio believes that there is an "unconscious factor" in the distinction between the legal treatment of male and female homosexuals. He believes that it lies in the fact that the male ego refuses to believe that any woman could possibly secure sexual satisfaction without a man. "The tendency for judges not to prosecute female homosexuals," he writes, "perhaps is an unconscious expression of denying its existence."

A Greenwich Village lesbian I know, who dresses exclusively as a butch, told me she was bothered by the police only a few times, even though on a summer night in Washington Square "plenty goes on on the grass and the coppers know it." The few times a policeman did stop her, it was not to arrest her, but instead to force her into an empty garage, where he insisted she strip down before him while he examined her entire body for heroin capsules and marijuana cigarettes. "He only did it to butches," she said. "He must have got some kind of big kick out of it. If we tried to resist him, he'd say he'd turn and say that we were found in the act and we'd get our names on the record books. We didn't have any choice. But most of them let us alone. The fags are the ones the want. Fags make more trouble. Women are quieter and they don't want to start fights or squeal around in the streets after straight people."

The consensus seems to be that women homosexuals, although less likely to be arrested, are also less likely to give the police a reason for arresting them. Howard Whitman, in *Terror in the Streets*, a study of crime in the United States, says that because lesbians have "quieter" attachments, and because these attachments are usually marked by reasonable fidelity on the part of both partners, female homosexuals are not nearly the police problem that males are. Karpman, Kinsey, and Henry made similar observations. While I would perhaps quarrel with Whitman's choice of adjectives ("quieter"), I would certainly agree with him that lesbians seldom clash with the law, whereas male homosexuals frequently do.

Whitman adds to this observation a Lieutenant Morgan's comment upon those occasional "blatant female prowlers" with whom every police squad is familiar at some time or other. "I'm afraid some of the females aren't only as bad as men," Morgan says; "some of them are worse." He told of two female prowlers who were picked up in Pittsburgh one evening, were held over to await arraignment the following morning, and were caught one hour after their arrest in overt "unnatural" love-making right in the police station. Another of these prowlers was caught on a downtown Pittsburgh street openly and flagrantly propositioning women. Such female homosexuals are, in Whitman's words, "not just overt lesbians who hang around in slacks and masculine hairdos in the few 'queer' bars and night clubs which most cities have; but actual female prowlers who accost women and try to proselyte girls quite as vilely as men prowl after other men, and with quite the same possibilities of violence and murder."

While it is necessary for the safety of any community to have laws against those citizens who would willfully do harm to another, the law against sodomy under which the homosexual is punished is an outdated and outlandishly archaic law. As Dr. Benjamin Karpman describes it, it "goes back almost to Deuteronomy . . . and in the light of psychiatric knowledge of the past forty years, it seems to embody little else than ecclesiastical fury." Karpman goes on to say that the modernly oriented psychiatrist can see no reason why any law should prohibit any two adult persons from engaging in any form of sexual activity in private and by mutual consent.

"The recent furor over homosexuality," Karpman concludes, "was baseless, stupid, political, and productive of nothing except glorious encouragement of blackmail, which in the light of abstract morality, is the worst and most contemptible of all possible crimes."

In sharp contrast to the opinion that two adults ought to be allowed to choose any form for sexual activity they wish, providing they are not offensive and that they are in accord with one another, there is the opinion that the law should be sterner in its treatment of the homosexual. Dr. J. Paul de River, prominent Los Angeles criminologist and psychiatrist, has this to say in his book *The Sexual Criminal*:

> The homosexual, both male and female, presents a most difficult problem. . . . It has been the author's experience that in the majority of these cases, these individuals are very well satisfied with themselves, and few have any desire to overcome their perverse practices. Most of them are egotists, living under the idea that they can improve upon the laws of God and man. They disregard society, or what other people might think of them, and they will tell you that they are happy and are not doing any harm to anyone else.

Dr. de River then goes on to explain that the homosexual must be doing harm to normal people, for homosexuality is on the increase, and therefore the homosexual is not keeping his perversion to himself, but "contaminating someone else."

"It is the author's opinion," he adds, "that the homosexual is a psychopath rather than a neurotic. In a certain sense, we might say that they are delusional, but this does not in any way mean that they don't know what they're doing or that they're not responsible for their actions. Tolerance of our social order towards this form of perversion has not helped matters."

Dr. Karpman and Dr. de River are contemporaries, and both reflect contemporary and conflicting attitudes toward homosexuality and the law. It will probably be a good many years before the statutes of the various states realize any innovation. Meanwhile, it is the homosexual's plight to live by and around the law of sodomy. Because the law is more theoretical than practical, and because it is not often enforced save in those instances that involve attempted seduction of a heterosexual by a homosexual, or open, overt promiscuous "prowling," or seduction of the young, it is not a law that outrages most homosexuals. When it does concern the homosexual, it is more often the male whom it concerns, for the male is most often confronted with it. The lesbian enjoys greater freedom.

"I never think of the actual law," one lesbian said, "because I just really don't believe anyone *I* know would be affected by it. But I do think of the law in symbolic ways. Most particularly in lines of poetry, like that one by Housman. Have you read it?" She quoted the first verse for me:

Oh who is that young sinner with the handcuffs on
    his wrists?
And what has he been after that they groan and
    shake their fists?
And wherefore is he wearing such a conscience-
    stricken air?
Oh they're taking him to prison for the colour of his
    hair. . . .

"When I read things like that," she said, "that's about the only time I give much thought to the, quote, law, unquote. . . . And you?" she asked.

I had to admit that I was not greatly concerned either, nor were any of my homosexual friends of whom I could think.

13.   CAN A LESBIAN BE CURED?

Today medical science is convinced that homosexuality is not a condition caused by biological or hereditary factors. It is regarded as a psychogenic disorder. Therefore, when the lesbian seeks treatment, the method of treatment must be a psychological one.

Of the lesbians with whom I am acquainted, only three are undergoing serious and intensive analysis. From time to time I have encountered female homosexuals who have flirted with psychoanalysis for a brief but futile period, during which they became dissatisfied with their progress, or with what they considered to be a lack of progress. Included in this category are the lesbians who consult "therapists," "lay analysts," and various and sundry "practitioners" of psychology and pseudo psychology, hoping to find some quick and cheap way of solving their problems, or merely relieving their periodic anxieties.

The three analysands whom I know are quite distinct types, and it may be of interest to describe them.

Iris is a transvestite who goes under the name of Rick in gay circles. A male impersonator in a Greenwich Village night club, she is in her third year of psychoanalysis. Her principal topic of conversation is her experiences on the couch.

"My main reason for wanting to be cured," she told me, "is my fear of old age. What'll become of me when I'm forty or fifty? How long can I hold down a job where I can wear these clothes? I just can't bear female garb, and the future scares the hell out of me!"

Iris visits her analyst four times a week at a cost of $240 a month, which is approximately half of her monthly earnings, including tips.

Millie is thirty-three, four years older than Iris. She manages a small bookshop, and has lived alone since her breakup with a lesbian who was her roommate for close to five years. Millie never frequents homosexual haunts, dates men occasionally, and considers the mention of her analysis very embarrassing. She has three sessions a week at a cost of $180 a month. This would be financially impossible for her were it not for a running bank loan. She is entering her fourth year of analysis. When we discussed the lesbian's chances for cure through psychoanalysis once, Millie said she didn't know what her chances were, but anything was better than the misery she had experienced in an overt lesbian relationship. Her only experience with a male was an unsuccessful one during her teens, which hurt her physically. She has been frigid with men since then.

Lou is a stunning model in her late twenties. She is kept by a wealthy married man, whose Christmas gift to her three years ago was the money for psychoanalytic treatment. A bisexual who prefers homosexuality, but sees no chance for happiness in such a relationship, Lou describes her analytic experience as "the greatest thing since the talkies." In a more serious vein she declares that since she has been visiting the analyst she has fewer fits of depression, and her suicidal thoughts have disappeared. Lou has never lived with another lesbian, but she has had numerous two- or three-month affairs with girls. She goes to the doctor six days a week, and it costs her boy friend $450 a month.

While it is impossible for the layman to speculate accurately as to an individual's chances for cure in psychoanalysis,

I would guess that of these three girls, Millie has perhaps the best opportunity. Iris wants to be cured supposedly because she fears growing older, and not so much because she is presently unhappy or discouraged with what she is. Indeed, Iris makes her living as a result of what she is, and that job in turn supports her analysis, which is a favorite conversation piece for her. In addition, the opinion is held by many psychoanalysts that transvestitism is one of the most difficult things to treat. In the book *The Homosexuals*, edited by Krich, in the essay on "Transvestitism" it is said that "as far as is known, all attempts at treating genuine cases of transvestitism have been futile, provided treatment is taken to mean attempts at curing the affliction." Because Iris does not want to learn to live with the being she now is, but to change into a woman who can wear dresses comfortably, her chances for cure are probably slim.

Lou, on the other hand, while less badly off than Iris, is not particularly well off, either, in terms of ultimate cure. First, Lou states emphatically that her preference is homosexual, and that she turns from it only because she cannot see a chance for happiness, yet she is currently not unhappy in her homosexual affairs, so long as she has her weekly psychiatric sessions to alleviate her guilt. Secondly, Lou was given analysis as a gift, and the majority of analysts will readily agree that the patient gets the most from psychoanalytic treatment when he or she has had to sacrifice somewhat in order to be helped. When a person sacrifices, he has a need for that for which he sacrificed, and the need to be made well is the major prerequisite of successful psychoanalytic treatment. "It is claimed that a willingness to be cured is halfway to health," Robert Caprio wrote in *Female Homosexuality*. "This particularly applies to lesbians. The prognosis therefore is a favorable one wherever there exists this genuine wish to be helped."

Of the three lesbians, Millie's prognosis is probably the

most favorable. Unhappy as a homosexual to the point where she must manipulate her budget tightly in order to seek help, Millie is not particularly proud of the fact that she is being analyzed. Most serious analysands aren't. Sickness is not something in which the average person takes pride. Neither does Millie persist in her homosexual relationship, or seek out other homosexuals, any more than a heart case overexerts. Her desire for cure is genuine.

Supposing that a lesbian has such a genuine desire for cure, what are the chances that she will actually be cured? Freud was quite skeptical about a cure for inversion. Writing on "A Case of Homosexuality in Women," he said that it would be "premature or a harmful exaggeration if at this stage we were to indulge in hopes of a 'therapy' of inversion that could be generally used." He added, "Any analogous treatment of female homosexuality is at present quite obscure." Today, however, few analysts would be pessimistic with regard to curing the lesbian, provided this lesbian really wanted to be a heterosexual instead of a homosexual.

Stekel, who followed Freud in theory for the most part, disagreed quite radically with him on this point. The first condition Stekel laid down for an adequate cure of homosexuality, which he was certain could be accomplished—and in fact did accomplish himself for his patients—was that the patient gain adequate self-knowledge. Stekel believed that over a goodly period of time the physician must work diligently to help the patient to avoid sidetracking, and stubbornly overlooking certain facts of his nature and his experience that were pertinent to his mental health. To bring these things into the field of consciousness, Stekel said, was no simple task. It is an achievement challenging the whole medical art, "requiring insight, diplomacy, sympathy, friendliness, and patience."

Once the patient is aware of his bisexuality and once he sees the causes of his homosexual leaning, the analyst has accomplished half or three-fourths of his task. "Beyond this point," Stekel writes, "the patient must help himself. If he is truly earnest about his desire to get well, he will accomplish it without being pushed to it. If he truly lacks the will, the situation is hopeless in spite of analysis."

Stekel stated that a cure could be claimed only when the subject under treatment was able to fall in love with a suitable person of the other sex. Too often, he thought, a patient claiming that he or she could have orgasms in sexual relations with the opposite sex considered this evidence of cure.

"He must also learn to recognize the essential unity of erotism and sexuality. Only when the homosexual finds it possible to fix his erotism and sexuality upon the same goal, in a person of the opposite sex—in other words, when he learns to love in adult manner—have we the right to claim a cure. . . ."

Most psychiatrists, psychologists, and psychoanalysts would agree that the cure for lesbianism is accomplished only when the lesbian looks for her whole fulfillment to the opposite sex. In direct opposition to this theory, however, is a conditional theory that the lesbian, in some instances, can realize adjustment only in a homosexual relationship. In such a case, the analyst's task is to enable the patient to accept homosexuality by helping her to overcome guilt, fear, and frustration. While this is not commonly ascribed to by psychoanalysis today, neither is it a rare or infrequent phenomenon. Helene Deutsch, in her book *Psychology of Women*, describes her experience with a patient whom she liberated from a condemnation of her homosexuality, making it possible for the patient to find happiness in an uninhibited homosexual affair. Explaining her feelings about such a treatment, Dr. Deutsch wrote:

> It goes without saying that the experience fell far below what psychoanalysis demands of an adult person . . . But sometimes the therapeutic goal can be

achieved only through compromise. In this case analytic treatment did not lead to the patient's renouncing homosexuality and turning toward men; thus its
real task was not fulfilled. But it succeeded in bring-
ing the unhappy woman, who was constantly on the
verge of suicide, to a point where . . . she could
achieve tenderness and sexual gratification. A better
solution . . . proved impossible.

If it is true that a lesbian can be cured once she sincerely
desires cure, it is probably not true that there are very many
lesbians who seek treatment. In Karpman's study of the sexual
offender he stated that "women homosexuals, as a group, are
more psychopathic than men homosexuals and do not seek
treatment as eagerly or as frequently as the male homosexual."
In addition to the obvious explanations that women are (a)
more inhibited and thus more reluctant to put their sexual
feelings into words before a doctor, or (b) sometimes less
aware of guilt in a homosexual affair because of the greater ease
they enjoy in their relationships as compared with the male,
there is another consideration in the case of the lesbian who
does not seek treatment. That is the fact that psychoanalysis,
even an inexpensive one, is commonly far too expensive for
the average working woman or girl. The male is better paid, as
a rule, and usually better able to "live on nothing," as I heard
one male say of himself when describing his financial situation
since starting analysis. Of course, it might be more accurate
still to say that the majority of people, male or female, cannot
afford the intense years-long psychoanalysis that the homosexual must anticipate if he or she desires cure.

There is one more reason for a lesbian's failure to seek
treatment: She does not want to be different. Sometimes one
of these types goes through a brief period when she thinks she
might like to change, and attends one or two analytic sessions,

or talks constantly of beginning analysis "one of these days," but more often the "incurable" lesbian is content to believe either that there is no other way or that even if there is, she does not want it.

The "incurable" lesbian as I have known her is not usually the tragic heroine of a lesbian novel who lives in abject misery, nor is she the psychotic case material in some psychiatrists' files. While I hesitate to say that she is a thoroughly happy person, at the same time I cannot in all honesty adjudge her to be an unhappy person. The overt lesbian is generally simply another human being with her share of problems and neuroses, no worse off really than many heterosexuals who must inevitably cope with his various moods, maladies, and maladjustments in life. There are exceptions, of course, and unfortunately it is quite frequently these exceptions that society hears about or sees. While overt homosexuality can never be considered a normal condition, it is an abnormality that does not necessarily have to be offensive to society or offending in society. As Dr. Clara Thompson wrote in an essay called "Changing Concepts of Homosexuality in Psychoanalysis," "An overt homosexual way of life can play a constructive role or a destructive role in the personality. It may be the best type of human relation of which a person is capable and as such is better than isolation."

The answer to the question "Can the lesbian be cured?" is similar to the answer the mother of a little boy gave when he asked her, "Can I go swimming at the pond?"

"Yes," she said, "you can. But you may not."

The lesbian can be cured; many of them have been. But unless she really wants to be cured, she may not be. It is solely up to her to grant permission for a treatment that will ultimately be successful.

14.   HERE COMES THE BRIDE

The shower for Elsa was held on a warm June evening the Wednesday before her wedding to George. The small flat in the West Twenties was filled with a score of well-wishers, all friends of the bride, all lesbians. Elsa was making the break. She was renouncing gay life for marriage, and everyone present was rejoicing with her. Thirtyish and rather attractive, a lesbian who had enjoyed and suffered through many homosexual affairs, Elsa had first met George in the restaurant where she was a hostess. As she grew to like him and feel comfortable with him, she gradually began to tell him more and more about herself. George was fifteen years her senior, a big, quiet salesman, lonely and sympathetic, and very much in love with Elsa. Eventually she introduced him to her lesbian friends, and George was considered a "good sport" and a "swell guy" by all of them. When he asked Elsa to marry him and go to Chicago to live with him, raise a family, and try for a fresh start, Elsa was sure that this would be the answer to long years of drifting aimlessly and endlessly on a sea as sad as it was gay.

"I'm sick and tired of not having anyone or anything that's permanent—that's mine—that I can count on!" she said. "I want roots! I don't care if I ever make love to another woman, if I can only find an anchor in this life."

The girls at the shower all agreed with Elsa.

"You're lucky to get out of this rat race," one said.

"They don't come any better than George," said another.

"I wish I could do it! I wish I could make the break!" cried a third.

A butch laughed. "Years from now when you're back visiting New York and pushing a baby carriage down the street, you and I will come face to face, and you'll look right through me, honey. You'll be so straight you won't even see me."

"I won't forget my old friends," Elsa protested.

The butch said, "That's just what you will do if you're smart, Elsa. This is your chance for a real life. We'll be cheering you on, honey, but don't you take any bows when we applaud from the side lines. Don't you even let on you know we exist."

Everyone at Elsa's shower made her feel that she was doing the right thing. As she opened gift after gift and viewed the raw material with which she was to build a new life as a housewife in Chicago, she seemed to revel in her new role. Indeed, it was as though already Elsa had changed, grown a little apart from these people feting her. When George arrived, toward the end of the evening, she ran to him, her arms filled with copper frying pans, wooden salad bowls, and salt and pepper shakers, and she cried, "Look, darling—isn't it all wonderful? It's for our home! Home, George! It sounds beautiful, that word. Home!"

It was understood that the only people present at the wedding were to be George's and Elsa's family. Some of her gay friends stood outside the church and watched as she emerged, beaming and bright with happiness. The bride and groom caught a plane that evening, and after that Elsa wrote only three postcards to her old crowd.

The first arrived within a week. She and George had found a wonderful apartment. It had a sunken living room and a view of the lake, and they were going to furnish it themselves. The gifts she had received would come in so handy! She sent many, many thanks. There was no return address.

The second arrived in late September. Chicago, she said, had just as many gay bars as New York had, but they weren't so much fun. George and she had made the rounds on the gay circuit one night, "just for fun, *of course*." What was the news back home? Please write. There was a return address.

The third arrived in December. It said simply: "Round up the kids; tune up the brass band. The prodigal daughter returns two days before Christmas—*alone*!"

Elsa is not untypical of many lesbians who try to make the break from homosexuality to a more stable existence in a heterosexual world. The desire to escape from the rootless routine of lesbian life is a common one, particularly for those lesbians who have passed from their twenties into their thirties. The fear of age, and the realization that from thirty on there is less and less chance of escaping this microcosm of abnormality, many times compels the lesbian to grasp at straws, hang on, and hope to be towed out of the mire.

What is this mire to which some lesbians feel marriage is the antidote? For Elsa, it was a hopeless situation in which she was forever going with and breaking up with females as unsure of themselves and insecure as she was.

A permanent relationship between homosexuals is a difficult accomplishment. The dream of a younger, less experienced lesbian that one day she will find her perfect mate and live in a homosexual "marriage" with her becomes more and more ephemeral each year. Many lesbians stay together for from one to ten years; some stay together longer; but few stay together permanently. Youth enjoys freedom of the "no strings attached" kind, but age brings anxiety about the future and about the "someone" who will be there to share that future. While the divorce rate among the general populace is large, in most instances marriage viewed from outside seems to be a permanent anchor in life, a way of being in a world of one's own within the large and frightening world of all peoples.

Many lesbians, unlike Elsa, who traveled in gay circles, do not find it easy to establish a new relationship, once an old relationship is severed. Those who shy from homosexual haunts and have no homosexual friends do not know where to look for the love they need. Frustrated and lonely, envious of the heterosexual world, where love can be sought with a fair amount of abandon, some lesbians begin to hate themselves. Coupled with that self-hatred is the fear of missing out on life altogether. Marriage seems better than nothing, and if a man comes along at a moment when such a lesbian is suffering from this feeling of isolation, she may see in him her release from loneliness. Sometimes she will confide in him that she has been a homosexual (usually being careful to use the past tense); just as often she will never tell him.

Such a lesbian was Chris. Publicity director of a charity organization, thirty-four, and recently broken off from a nine-year lesbian relationship with a dancing instructor, Chris was miserable. While she dated several men, she was not sexually aroused by them, although she had relations with them and feigned orgasm. Knowing no other homosexuals, Chris was as addicted to hope as an alcoholic is to liquor. Each new woman she encountered whom she found attractive was a "possibility" in Chris's thinking. Many times she became a close friend of one, seeing her constantly—at lunch, for movies, for cock-tails—even double-dating with her. Chris would search her eyes for some spark of recognition, some sign that the woman could feel as Chris did. Every gesture the woman made, every word she spoke, all of her actions were scrutinized by Chris. Hope sprang eternal in her heart that one day a woman would react to her as a lover.

Chris was always careful. She knew the dangers. She swore she would never make the first move. Then one evening at an office party, when everyone was very drunk, a young secretary put her arms around Chris and kissed her neck. Chris invited her immediately to her apartment, and there promptly made homosexual advances. The girl was horrified. She had been very intoxicated, and she had admired Chris as her superior in the office. Flattered that Chris had invited her to her place, she went along. But she was not a homosexual, and when Chris revealed herself to her, it was humiliating, embarrassing, and sordid for both girls.

The day after the party Chris applied for three weeks' leave. She packed her bags and went on a vacation to a dude ranch. Upon her return she announced that she was going to marry a young man she had met there. In less than three weeks Chris was a bride. Her husband, in his mid-twenties, and not particularly sophisticated, had been swept off his feet by Chris. He knew nothing about her homosexuality until many months after they were married, when drunkenly one evening during an argument Chris blurted it out. Even so, it made no difference to her husband, and they remained married for approximately seven months after that evening. When a year had passed, Chris got a divorce. She simply did not love the man, and, living with him day after day, she was beginning to resent him and dislike him. Today's Chris is friendly with her ex-husband, and she is much the same woman she was before her marriage, save for the fact that she drinks a little more than she used to, and claims to be saving her money for psychoanalysis.

"The one thing I want in this world I can't have," a lesbian friend complained to me. "A child! Even if I could find a guy and work up a deal so that he'd get me pregnant and then leave, I know I'm not fit to be a mother."

Many homosexuals are not convinced that motherhood is not for them. Their desire for a child is stronger than their perspective is rational. How often I have heard a lesbian claim that were she to marry and have children, she would not need women! Her children would be all she would need. She would be a good mother, better than many, she insists, because she would have so much more love to give. Needless to say, this reason for marriage on the part of the lesbian is another poor one, but it is not difficult to sympathize with the homosexual woman in this matter. Despite her abnormality, she is still a female, and as a female she has the feminine wish to produce offspring. A very masculine lesbian whom I know married a good friend who understood her plight and was willing to live with her as her husband and the father of her children. He was a little, soft-faced, skinny man who worked as a bookkeeper, and he did not have many acquaintances or any particular interest in life until his marriage. Corky, the lesbian, truly respected the man she married, even though there was no sexual interest on her part. Her husband, on the other hand, enjoyed Corky's apathy toward him, and oddly enough, found it stimulating. They have been married for nearly six years, and Corky has had two boys. While I do not know whether or not Corky has given up homosexual adventuring altogether, I do know that she is a busy, energetic, and enthusiastic wife, as well as an extremely affectionate mother. The family unit seems quite close and contented.

Corky was lucky. Few lesbians have a true male friend, much less one who would agree to such a marriage and revel in his wife's frigidity.

Sometimes lesbians marry to mask their abnormality.

"I'd just like to get married so I could have a Mrs. before my name," I heard a lesbian say. "That would solve everything for me, to say nothing of how it would please my family."

Frequently lesbians marry for economic gains. A lesbian, much more than a male homosexual, can simulate orgasm and sexual response so that her husband may be deluded into thinking that she is a normal woman. Although the marriage probably will not last any great length of time, it is not unlikely that she may sue for support, or that support may be offered her as a means of terminating the marriage. In one case that a lawyer told me about, a lesbian married a man whom she later tantalized by saying to him, "I'd rather have a woman than you any time!" While she never refused him his husband's right of sexual relations, she stopped feigning pleasure and openly ridiculed his technique. She would not consent to a divorce unless he paid stiff alimony, and feeling that this was unfair, the husband sought the lawyer's advice about the possibility of getting a divorce on grounds of misrepresentation. This however, was not a valid reason, he was informed, nor was homosexuality—even if she were to have relations with another woman—cause for suit. When ultimately he sought out another woman for the warmth and love his wife denied him, his wife had him followed by detectives until she obtained concrete evidence of adultery. She won her divorce suit, and was granted a sizable alimony, despite references in court to the husband's difficult plight. Adultery, as far as the law is concerned, is still the greatest sin in marriage.

In rare instances lesbians meet and marry male homosexuals. A "front marriage" of this sort is probably the most successful of any that a lesbian might make with a man. "Front marriages" ward off suspicion, offer companionship and a home, and occasionally provide children for two people who would otherwise be unable to form their own family ties. I know of only one such marriage, although mention is often made of them in novels and other literature dealing with homosexuality.

Andy and Jill, the couple with whom I am acquainted, are both overt homosexuals. They have one child, a daughter. The only times they had sexual relations with each other were those times when they were attempting to make Jill pregnant. They do not enjoy heterosexual relations. Throughout the five years of their marriage they have had one rule: Don't foul the nest! In other words both have promised never to bring their lovers to the apartment they share. Besides this, they have agreed to be discriminate and discreet in their homosexual relations, and to keep all conversation concerning them from the ears of Patty, their child. Relatively well adjusted in this "front marriage," they have managed to live with each other in a comfortable, affectionate, friendly fashion, and Patty seems to be a typical happy four-year-old. Andy and Jill feel that Patty is not any worse off than many youngsters, despite her perverse parents. Both adore her, provide well for her, and spend a large amount of time with her.

"It isn't an ideal situation for a child, I suppose," Jill said, "but what child is raised in an ideal situation? We love Patty—she's ours. If our homosexuality ever hurts her, it'll be because either Andy or I have been untrue to our rules. Patty need never know, we feel."

If "front marriages" are more successful than any other kind of marriage for the lesbian, they are probably more difficult to arrange. Lesbians, as a rule, seem to have some of that disdain for the male homosexual that he seems to have for her, and they seldom intermingle or mix socially. Those lesbians who do not patronize gay places or have a circle of homosexual friends do not frequently encounter a male homosexual often enough to become friendly with him. When a lesbian and a male homosexual do become friends, it is not often that both have a keen desire to get married. Donald Webster Cory, in his discussion of such marriages among homosexuals, says that the male homosexual, if he were to want a wife, probably would not choose a lesbian. "The . . . Lesbian," he writes, "by her very nature, seldom arouses the response of warmth, affection, self-confidence, that the gay youth, although not necessarily an escape-seeker, nevertheless desires from marriage. Finally, he cannot actually visualize the Lesbian as a likely homemaker, wife and mother." This is an interesting observation in view of the fact that it was written by a male homosexual, and illustrates the slight scorn for the lesbian which most male homosexuals have. While, as a homosexual, he would consider himself a good husband for a normal woman, he would not consider the lesbian a fit person to be his wife.

The lesbian, then, may want to married for many reasons, from security to motherhood to a "front." The lesbian bride is not a rare phenomenon. Two lesbians in England recently made their own somewhat imaginative attempt at solving the dilemma. The following story was published in the *New York World-Telegram and Sun* on Monday, December 13, 1954:

Greenwich, England, Dec. 13—Two young newly-weds were fined today on grounds both were women.

"There is more to marriage than the physical side," pleaded the "bridegroom," Violet Ellen Kathrine Jones, 26.

She posed as a bachelor named Victor Eric Kenneth Jones in order to marry Joan Mary Lee, 21.

The government said Miss Jones was not a man and therefore charged her and her "bride" under the perjury act of 1911 with making a false statement for the purpose of being wrongly listed in the marriage register.

Conviction today broke up the two-month-old "marriage" of Violet and Joan, and cost each $70 in fines.

"I am a man," Miss Jones told police who brought the charge. "But if you mean physically, I still possess female organs. I have been to doctors to alter my sex, but I got tired of waiting."

Miss Jones looked masculine in court today, wearing a blue businessman's suit and with her hair cut short and parted on the side. But when she pleaded guilty, her voice sounded suspiciously high.

Her wife was with her, dressed becomingly in a green dress and bottle green coat. She also pleaded guilty.

15.   A WORD TO PARENTS

As a parent, try for a moment to imagine yourself in the situation I am going to describe. You are the mother of a seventeen-year-old girl. Late one night a storm arises and you go into your daughter's room to check the windows. A close friend of your daughter's is spending the week end with her, and as you enter, in the light shining into the room from the hall, you are witness to a scene that leaves you speechless and drenched with perspiration.

You return to your room and try to erase it from your memory. You try to sleep, believing you will see things more clearly in the morning. But nothing works. You can't forget and sleep won't come. The word "lesbian" sticks in your throat, and you search your heart, and the memories of the long years you have raised your daughter, hoping to come up with evidence that will disprove the meaning of what you saw. You want to believe that it was a nightmare, a horrible phantasy, a bizarre mirage—but the fact stands, and the image of your daughter and her friend indulging in passionate love-making is engraved on your mind.

You have never had the slightest doubt that your little girl was anything but normal, happy, a typical teen-ager. It is incredible that such a thing could happen in your family. You are shocked, sick, outraged, ashamed, and horrified.

What are you going to do?

Should you consult a psychiatrist, a minister—someone who can talk to your daughter and try to help her? Is it possible for the three of you to sit down and discuss it rationally together? Should you wait until the other girl has left, and then punish your daughter, scold her, or attempt to make her see the seriousness of the situation? Should you buy her some sort of book to read about homosexuality, and hope it will guide her into an intelligent appreciation of homosexual manifestations and psychology? Or would it be better to ignore the matter, and pray to God that she will grow out of it, or meet a boy she will fall in love with, or somehow cope with her problem in her own way? She is seventeen, no longer a child, but she is still your child. What is right, wise, intelligent, in such a situation?

Because parents as individuals differ so greatly in personality, psychology, and emotion, the "right thing to do" probably cannot be ascertained. Some mothers and fathers are inarticulate or overly emotional in the face of problems that concern their children. Many times only one of the parents is truly able to talk with a child and "reach" her. A few times neither parent has established a relationship with their child that enables her or them to feel that confidences and delicate subjects can be discussed openly and freely. Often the child is of a nature that makes it humiliating or embarrassing for her to be approached by either or both parents about anything relating to sexual matters. Despite the way in which parents have tried to bring up their children, not uncommonly they will discover that their daughter is a complete enigma to them, a person whom they love dearly, laugh and cry with often, but understand seldom.

The only thing that can perhaps be decided upon in an instance such as this is what is not the right thing to do. In *Female Homosexuality*, Robert Caprio explains that although homosexuality is neither desirable nor acceptable in our society, "experimental conduct" happens sufficient times to deserve careful understanding and handling, rather than violent denunciation. Teen-agers should not be made to feel guilty or depraved because of a homosexual experience. Often it is part of growing up, and just as often it has a tendency to fade naturally by itself. A parent who discovers that a daughter is involved in a homosexual relationship can be assured of one basic fact: No girl has ever had homosexuality beaten out of her, nor has she been led into heterosexuality by being punished for homosexuality, disowned because of it, or labeled unnatural, queer, lesbian, or degenerate as a result of it.

The mother of a girl with whom I went to boarding school handled the problem of her daughter's homosexual inclinations in a rather unique and insidiously brutal way. While the girl was home for spring vacation, the mother came upon a package of love notes from a Helen C. in the girl's suitcase. This same Helen C. had been making long-distance calls from her home to her daughter every evening. Overhearing one or two, the mother noted that the conversation was "mushy." Saying nothing to her daughter, the mother waited until the week end, when she was having people over for cocktails and dinner. The mother knew that another long-distance call would come through at seven that evening, and that her daughter would have to receive it at the house's only phone, in the living room. She called her daughter into her room and said, "Look, Marilyn, I realize what's going on between you and Helen. It's your life—I can't live it for you. But I want to make one thing clear. I would be embarrassed to tears if any of my friends suspected that my daughter was a lesbian. So when your girl friend calls this evening, I am going to say that you're not in. Everyone will be in the living room, and I'd be humiliated to have any of my guests overhear your lovey-dovey conversation with Helen."

Marilyn was fifteen at the time. It had never occurred to

her that she was a lesbian. Such things simply don't occur to young girls who live in a manless world and love their class-mates, even when that love is physical. While Marilyn's mother did not try to punish her or separate her from Helen or denounce her indignantly or even threaten her, her selfish han-dling of the situation high-lighted two facts for Marilyn: Her mother did not care what she did or what she was, so long as it did not affect her own reputation, and she was unqualifiedly labeled a lesbian, without ever having discussed the meaning of homosexuality or its manifestations with her mother.

When Marilyn returned to school, she stopped her friend-ship with Helen abruptly, and for many months stuck to her-self, depressed, nervous, and tearful. In June, as everyone left for summer vacation, Marilyn did the one thing she thought would expiate her "crime." Both of us were going south on the same train. The cars were filled with soldiers, sailors, and marines, and as the Pullman porter made up our berths, Mar-ilyn and I talked with two sailors and drank whisky from their flasks. I got horrible ill, but somehow managed to get into my upper berth before I passed out. When I awoke the following morning, I could not find Marilyn, and when I looked into the berth assigned to her, I saw that it was unmade. Hours later I found her sobbing in the ladies' room. Before bewil-dered women brushing their teeth and making up their faces, Marilyn sobbed out the whole story to me—her mother's words, the phone call she could not take, the months of forc-ing herself to avoid Helen, and ultimately her sordid experi-ence on the train home, in a roomette with a sailor.

I don't know what ever became of my classmate. She did not return to school the following year, and none of us heard from her. The last time I saw her, one of the women who had overheard her near hysterical story was trying to find out if there were time for Marilyn to take a douche before the train pulled into Louisville.

"I just don't want to be pregnant," Marilyn was sobbing, and the woman was shaking her head despairingly and muttering something about war ruining people's lives.

War is sometimes kinder on individuals than the experience of growing up is. War kills, war makes you hungry for food, homeless, and deprived of your loved ones. But war is something you know everyone is going through and enduring, and the major and minor tragedies a youngster suffers through seem to be unique to her. "Nobody knows the troubles I've seen, nobody knows but Jesus" for many youngsters becomes "Nobody knows the troubles I've seen—nobody, not even Jesus." She dies many times, but still she lives. Her hunger is a hunger for love, and while she may live in a house with her parents, if she is not receiving that love she so requires, she may be as homeless as a waif.

The whole question of sex to a young girl is a perplexing one, and one that quite often causes great embarrassment, fear, and shame. If normal sexual activity is something that this young girl has not yet been able completely to accept and understand, one can imagine how difficult it must be for her suddenly to be confronted with the knowledge that she is involved in something far more shameful—abnormal sex. Marilyn's mother presumed that if Marilyn wrote love notes and had "lovely-dovey" conversations with Helen, she must be quite aware of her situation and her inversion, but this presumption does not take into consideration the slowness with which the young girl perceives the meaning of things sexual.

The parental insult "Why don't you grow up!" might be reversed by the youngster to "Why don't you grow down?" Too many times parents can't grow down to their children, they can't be their children long enough to try to wonder how they would feel were they to receive the same treatment they are administering to them.

The parents who become aware that their young daughter

is involved in homosexual activity have no small problem on their hands. Anger, indignation, punishment, or commands cannot solve the problem. Counsel sought on the part of the parents from a doctor is probably the most sure step in the right direction. Homosexuality is a sickness, and symptoms of it might well be treated as symptoms of any other serious illness are—by consultation with an authority who is better able to suggest treatment. The danger here lies in going about this in a way that might make the girl feel guilty, morbid, "dirty," or bad. Depending upon the closeness or lack of it between the girl and her parents, and the circumstances under which the matter arose, it is well to remember that this sickness, perhaps above all others a child may have, is one that requires delicate handling and sympathetic understanding.

What of the daughter who is a practicing overt homosexual?

What of her parents' relationship with her, and their attitude toward her?

Needless to say, many parents of lesbians are never aware of their daughters' homosexuality. They need never face the problem of how to accept a homosexual daughter. But many other parents are quite aware of their daughters' inversion, and their reactions are in many instances a determining factor in their daughters' ability or inability to live as fully happy lives as they might.

"My folks know about me," a lesbian remarked one evening as a group of us were discussing this subject, "but they never mention it. I can't say they're happy about it, but they're resigned to it. I wouldn't want them to mention it, either. What would there be for me or them to say? It's all right the way it is. I go home. I love them. They love me. Life is never perfect."

"My folks know about me, too," another said. "That's why I don't go home. I used to, but I finally couldn't take the snide remarks. My mother'd tell me about all the kids I grew up with who were married, and then she'd say, 'I don't know what I did wrong that made you what you are,' and she'd cry. My father'd get mad at me and say look what I've done to my mother, look how unhappy I've made her. I used to hate them and myself. Now I just send them Christmas cards and remember their birthdays. . . . I think they prefer it, but just the same, it's hard. I'm the only kid, and they're my only mom and dad."

A third lesbian said that her father did not allow her in the house, but that when he was gone she sneaked over to see her mother. "Mom always asks me who I'm rooming with—that's the way she puts it—and I tell her. Then she says, 'Is she a good person? Does she earn a decent living and go to church?' That's the most we ever say about it. Both of them know full well what I am. When I was sixteen my pop caught me in our living room with a girl, and he told me to get the hell out of his sight after he blackened both my eyes. I remember he said, 'Why don't you fight like a man if that's what you want to be so bad?' I still have dreams about him coming at me that way, nightmares when I wake up crying."

Most people, normal or abnormal, have trouble with their families. Few of us were blessed with all-understanding parents.

The sad fact in the lesbian's relationship with her family, and vice versa, is that the family trouble, if it is centered around the daughter's homosexuality, is not easily discussed, argued out, or compromised. If mention is made of it, it is often made via a nasty innuendo, a cruel criticism, or a persistent cry of "What did I do wrong?" on the part of the parent. It is pretty well established by psychiatrists and psychologists that the parent did do something wrong. Dr. Benjamin Karpman wrote, "Abnormal sex behavior derives from the unwholesome family atmosphere in which the child develops. The fault lies with the parents who themselves are products of unhealthy repressions."

Be this as it may, we can see an endless chain of blame, then, for homosexuality. It was the parents' fault, but it was their parents' fault that it was, and it was their parents' parents' fault, ad infinitum. The point to be made in a situation where the damage is done, and the lesbian is a lesbian, completely, irrevocably, overtly, is that regardless of whose fault it is that she is a homosexual, blame does not alter anything for her now. Self-abnegation on the part of either parent before the lesbian can only serve to make relations all the more uncomfortable. The best thing that can be done, probably, is to accept her situation, and to refer to it as little as one would to the sex life of a normal son or daughter. Discretion is not a difficult accomplishment, but the realization of the need for discretion often seems to be.

In his book on lesbianism Robert Caprio quotes some wise words from Dr. Shailor Lawton. In the hope that more parents will become aware of ways to *prevent* the development of inversion in their daughters, rather than waiting to cope with it after it has made itself manifest, I give them here:

> If we are ever able to solve the enigma of female homosexuality, we shall have to begin in the home. When daughters receive security of affection from their mothers, they will be less likely to seek it later in life with substitute mothers. Understanding that, we should never condemn the women who have surrendered to homosexuality. We should do what we can to help them. And we should—above all—try to *prevent* new recruits to their ranks by helping to make parents understand how important their love is to their daughters' future happiness.

16.   LOOKING FORWARD

Is homosexuality becoming a greater threat to society than it has ever been before? Is it on the increase? Is society going to be forced eventually to change its attitude toward the homosexual, and remove its laws discriminating against the homosexual? Is the increasing enlightenment on the part of the public with regard to the phenomenon of homosexuality making people more lenient, less lenient, or too lenient? What conclusions can we reach with regard to the position that the homosexual will occupy in the community in future years?

Homosexuality can be a threat to society in the event that an overt homosexual seduces a youth. "An experienced lesbian in seducing a young innocent girl," Robert Caprio wrote, "may seriously affect the girl's normal development of her sex life. In this respect lesbians are essentially sick individuals." While this is a consideration in the attitude society must assume with regard to the female homosexual and her right to exist without being discriminated against, it might be well to bear in mind one fact: Many more "young innocent girls" are seduced by heterosexuals than by homosexuals. In both cases the offender should pay the penalty for the crime. However, the fact that a woman is a lesbian does not mean that she is a potential seductress of young girls, any more than the fact that a man is a male means the same thing. A homosexual woman cannot be regarded as a threat to society because she might corrupt little girls. Anyone *might*.

One evening when I was discussing this with a young man, he said that it was not the possibility of lesbians' seducing children that made him view homosexuality as a great threat; it was something else.

"It's this," he said: "Everyone is screaming that we should let you people enjoy whichever sex you want to, that there shouldn't be any stigma attached to homosexuality. Well, suppose homosexuals *are* accepted. What I want to know is how many women would drift into it and stay with it? Nobody's going to censure them, so why not? What would become of the world then? How many kids would grow up to be perverts?"

While intelligent people are preaching tolerance of inversion they are not regarding the invert as a healthy person, nor are they classifying inversion along with heterosexuality as normal sexual activity. Therefore the answer to this young man's question, "How many kids would grow up to be perverts?" would probably be: "No more than do today." A permissive attitude toward homosexuality in no way infers that homosexuality is a desirable condition. It simply allows those people who are in the unfortunate position of being homosexual to live without stigma, until such time as science can eradicate or cure homosexuality in the human animal.

Meanwhile is homosexuality, as some believe, on the increase? Statisticians have not come up with definite figures proving that it is. Again, one can only speculate. It might be pertinent to consider the fact that one reason many people believe it is increasing is that information about the homosexual is becoming more easily available to the general public. As this public is more enlightened about it, mass media feeds its interests. Articles, plays, novels, and psychological studies of the subject appear, and people find themselves discussing homosexuality in the drawing room. In addition, many people who might previously have been close-mouthed about familiarity with the abnormality, or any experiences they might long ago have had with it, speak about it, admit it, or analyze it.

If homosexuality itself is not on the increase, mention of it among people today is far more prevalent than ever before. This is, indeed, a climate of concern with all things psychological.

What, then, will be society's attitude in the future toward the homosexual? What *should* be society's attitude toward the homosexual?

The latter question is more easily answered than the former. Benjamin Karpman states that "homosexuality is a condition for which the individual is no more responsible than he would be for tuberculosis, or high blood pressure." He attacks the position taken by "certain vociferous gentlemen, and echoed by the many newspapers, that homosexuals represent a serious threat to national security." This idea, he claims, can be applicable only to a very small percentage of such persons, who occupy positions in which they have access to secret information.

> It cannot possibly apply to the average government employee engaged in routine work that has no relation to policy-making issues. The crux of the argument revolves around the "particular susceptibility of homosexuals to blackmail." The proponents of this argument do not seem to realize that they are placing a premium on blackmail—the most despicable of all activities—and are deliberately inviting every unscrupulous policeman, and every vindictive and sadistic individual with a grudge, to engage in the very activity they are claiming as the basis for their discrimination against homosexuality.

Karpman believes that the blackmailing of homosexuals can be prevented only when homosexuality is accepted as a

fact and the unreasonable laws discriminating against it are
eradicated. The man who has given the best years of his life to
Civil Service, and who has been fired because of his sexual
abnormality, cannot easily secure other employment, and it
leaves him in the emotional position of Shylock, who said:

> Nay, take my life and all; pardon not that;
> You take my house when you do take the prop
> That doth sustain my house; you take my life
> When you do take the means whereby I live.

Less is said about lesbians' being removed from government
jobs in the homosexual purge. The majority of those employees
suffering this humiliation have been male homosexuals. Yet so
long as any law exists on the statute books that makes homosexuality in itself an offense, and so long as the homosexual is
looked upon as a security risk, the lesbian is not excluded from
the public's condemnation of the abnormal person.

What should society's attitude be?

Surely society ought to progress in its attitudes, to whatever extent possible, as quickly as the scientific world makes new
facts available. Science has never been in too great a hurry. By
comparison, however, the public is the turtle to the scientific
hare. Society should be aware by now that the lesbian is not a
depraved female, but the victim of a psychological orientation
that is different from the accepted social pattern. She may be
an intelligent and cultured woman, or she may be a stupid
fool, just as any normal woman may be. She may be a philan-
thropist or a thief, just as any normal women many be. Just
because she is a lesbian, she is not invested with any specific
character traits, other than her inversion. Society ought to recognize that lesbianism cannot be wiped out like the bubonic
plague. Society ought not to condemn or pity the homosexual, but simply to understand her.

What *will* be society's attitude toward the homosexual in the future?

In the 1920's Radclyffe Hall wrote her famous novel on female homosexuality, *The Well of Loneliness*. For its time, it was a most shocking novel. It ended with this plea:

"We have not denied You; then rise up and defend us. Acknowledge us, oh God, before the whole world. Give us also the right to our existence!"

At the same time in history, a doctor named Sigmund Freud was writing an essay entitled "The Psychogenesis of a Case of Homosexuality in a Woman." Science was already hard at work on the problem.

Since the twenties, the well of loneliness has been looked into by many authors, and their resulting novels have been received by the general public less and less with shock and disgust, more and more with interest and wonder. Freud's contribution of insight into the phenomenon of homosexuality has been enlarged, improved, and crystallized by a whole succession of psychologists and psychiatrists intent on understanding the homosexual being. The theatre and the movies have gradually found courage to dramatize the problems the homosexual faces. From the days when the homosexual was burned at the stake to the present day, when homosexuality can be studied, discussed, treated, and indulged in with discretion, is a big step. It has taken a long time, for society has short legs. There is still more distance to travel on this road to understanding. But thanks to science, mass media, and the growing receptivity on the part of all people toward learning, short legs may grow long, and big steps may seem small.

THE END

AFTERWORD
ANN ALDRICH AND LESBIAN WRITING IN THE FIFTIES

A book never arrives unaccompanied: it is a figure
against a background of other formations, depending on
them rather than contrasting with them.
    —Pierre Macherey, *A Theory of Literary Production*

The first paragraph of Ann Aldrich's *We Walk Alone* (1955) is
as shrewd as it is bold, taking the measure of conversations
about homosexuality and staking out a place within them.
Ann Aldrich situates *We Walk Alone* in what was then a growing field of writing by, for, and about gay people, while simul-
taneously pointing out that very little had been said about the
special historical and social development of lesbians and lesbian cultures. Aldrich writes:

> This book is the result of fifteen years of participation
> in society as a female homosexual. It is written with
> the conviction that there is a sincere need and
> demand for further enlightenment on this subject. I
> am convinced that the opinions and viewpoints of the
> lesbian herself are as valuable in arriving at conclu-
> sions about her nature as are those proffered by the

psychiatrist, sociologist, anthropologist, jurist, churchman, or psychologist." (xi)

Promising to supplement a wide range of literature written by
outsiders about homosexuality as well as to "give voice to
much of the opinion within this group" (xii), Aldrich
addressed a need for information that paradoxically had been
created by the very proliferation of professional opinions
about sexuality in general and homosexuality in particular.

By the mid 1950s, when *We Walk Alone* was published, it
was becoming easier to find written material, ranging from
sensational exposés to measured clinical studies about sexuality and its effects on mainstream cultural institutions. Indeed,
at the end of her book, Aldrich argues that "articles, plays,
novels, and psychological studies of the subject appear and
people find themselves discussing homosexuality in the drawing room. . . . If homosexuality itself is not on the increase,
mention of it among people today is far more prevalent than
ever before" (153). *We Walk Alone* entered a print market that,
while not saturated by books about homosexuality, was at the
very least able to accommodate a range of professionals or
"experts" in sexuality. Such experts, no matter what their professional credentials or their privately held social views, helped
to popularize the subject of sexuality and perhaps more impor-
tantly, helped to popularize the particular ways people imagined and discussed sexuality and sexual identities. Aldrich's
work situated itself at precisely the place where professional
assumptions and personal practices converged around female
sexuality. Part exposé, part ethnography, part vernacular sexology, *We Walk Alone* is nothing if not canny; it is deeply and
self-consciously immersed in multiple discussions about sexuality, and in its pages Aldrich adeptly traverses genres, texts,
and viewpoints. Its rhetorical sophistication makes it one of
the first lesbian texts to argue that gay and straight readers

alike need to understand that lesbianism was not something that happened to an individual woman. It was neither a psychological illness nor an ennobling if singular passion. Rather it was a culture, a whole way of life, as Raymond Williams has defined that term. Indeed, Aldrich goes a step further, revealing not one, but many lesbian cultures in her book (1989).

Despite the success her groundbreaking work enjoyed when it was published—*We Walk Alone* sold over a million copies and remained in print for over ten years (Meeker 2005a, 6)—Ann Aldrich has not yet enjoyed the success of her contemporaries who have been reclaimed by scholars and activists as important founders of a self-conscious lesbian and gay tradition. In part this is because a text like *We Walk Alone* is hard to categorize. Its intense engagement with multiple literary traditions and its deft manipulation of sometimes contradictory ways of understanding sexuality ironically make it a strangely singular text.

We can take the conditions of its publication as one example of its singularity. Published by Gold Medal/Fawcett, *We Walk Alone* can be considered a pulp, yet it bears only a nominal relationship to its more familiar lesbian pulp sisters. Neither fiction nor autobiography, it draws on narrative elements from each of those genres, and although it is neither a dramatic plea for acceptance nor a tortured confession, it borrows strategies from other texts that make precisely such appeals to their audiences. In many ways, Aldrich was able to cross certain boundaries that the pulps could not, even as she observed some of the publishing conventions that ensured that pulps could fly under the radar of obscenity laws. But crossing those boundaries also means that her narrative voice is unfamiliar. Aldrich's impatience with political pieties allows her a high tolerance for contradictions in voice, style, opinions, and practices. She is capable of analyses of individual lesbians that seem surprisingly conservative. She is capable of assessments of social conditions and prejudices that now seem refreshingly commonsensical. But it is precisely the unexpected, even queer, qualities of Aldrich's work that signal to us that her moment has finally come, for those qualities allow us to understand her as a pioneer in a new genre, whose ability to put together different textual styles and conventions seems to announce a more sophisticated and nuanced understanding of sexual identity as a complicated mixture of signs and conventions. Ann Aldrich is an important cultural historian, and her work can help us see anew a 1950s much queerer than we might have supposed.

The 1950s

Ann Aldrich's work is both an example of complicated mid-twentieth-century lesbian cultures as well as their first analyst. She is therefore not only an important literary "rediscovery"; she is an important resource for scholars interested in revisiting the Cold War era more generally. The 1950s have been too easily dismissed with a set of generalizations that create the very universalism they try to diagnose. That decade has been flattened in the popular imagination as a decade of conformity, populated by nuclear families which were unquestioningly invested in static, gender-rigid roles. Similarly, minority politics are popularly assumed to have been nascent, underdeveloped. But as historians and critics recast that era by looking at the political resistance to Cold War ideology, gay and lesbian historiography is following suit. Aldrich's work gives us a fifties in which gay subjects were not, in the formulation of influential gay historians "hidden from history," but who helped to shape a history that has not yet been fully appreciated. It is part of Aldrich's value that she diverges from what we think we know about the gay past, for these divergences show us a history filled with tantalizing possibilities of which our own moment represents only one.

Ann Aldrich's sharp-eyed humor, her attentiveness to the particulars of different social and geographic places in New York are revelatory of an historical moment richer than we imagined. In order to appreciate Aldrich's contributions, it's important to see her in three intersecting contexts, each of which may be organized around different kinds of "professional" or "expert" knowledge. Such knowledge is always partial, for it comes from experience; from the study of psychiatry, history, or literature; and from the sales records of publishers who sought to give their audiences what they seemed to want. Each of these represents a particular way of understanding the place of sexuality in culture, and they are thus important for Aldrich, who is dedicated to finding similarities between social spheres often kept rigidly apart in popular accounts of the era. Ann Aldrich may have walked alone, but she was writing in a crowded field.

First, it's important to see that Ann Aldrich wrote to and within a generalized, even stereotyped straight culture, trying to interest readers in the question of homosexuality (a question that was, as I shall show, much in the public's mind) as well as the professionals who sought to describe, diagnose, and perhaps more dangerously, to popularize specific ways of talking about homosexuality. These professionals were mainly from the straight world, but in at least one important instance, Aldrich addressed a gay man's professionally accredited ideas about how people should speak about (and what they should say about) gay life. Major mainstream periodicals and newspapers—*The Nation* and *Time* magazine—as well as many smaller magazines—like *The Mercury*—ended up enabling Aldrich to join the dialogue about how to discuss lesbianism. All had begun to carry stories on homosexuality directed to a mass audience.

Second, it's important to see that Aldrich was writing to and within a gay culture just beginning to organize politically and socially. That culture was, as she began to publish, just beginning to produce its own periodicals and to connect itself to a literary and historical tradition encompassing everything from pulp novels to the ancient Greeks. Central to this world were the periodicals produced by homophile organizations like the Daughters of Bilitis and the Mattachine Society. These periodicals enabled Aldrich as much as the mainstream periodicals did, for they also cleared a path for a lesbian to describe her own experiences to a general audience.

And finally, readers should recognize that Aldrich ended up reaching a more inchoate audience, one that might have been merely notional as she was writing the first of what would become a five-book Ann Aldrich series, but which materialized with surprising speed and force once the first book was published. This audience comprises those lesbians who were not organized, and who had not yet synthesized the contradictory and often frightening information about lesbianism they might have cobbled together. Ann Aldrich meant a great deal to such readers, and in a sense, recovering her lets us rediscover them too, their practices, their needs, and their desires. In a very material way, those readers left a trace in the historical record because they deluged Aldrich with letters after the publication of *We Walk Alone*, testifying to the extraordinary importance of the book as well as to the need that it filled.

The intersecting writers and publishing communities I examine had very different agendas, and addressed very different audiences, but it was not merely an interest in sexuality— and the sexualized woman in particular—that held them together. All understood the publication and circulation of books and ideas as an important and embattled enterprise. Censorship crises were rampant in the fifties and the publishing world we see through and within *We Walk Alone* was in many ways united over the value of public discussion, if not in agreement about the meaning of sexuality.

Meaker was in an enviable position in the early fifties; she may not have felt particularly lucky or well-compensated, and she might not have understood herself as central to the development of a specifically lesbian print network, but she was indeed at the center of it (see inside back cover for details). Indeed, we can consider Ann Aldrich herself as one of its most important developments. In the early fifties, Meaker worked as what she calls a "reader-secretary" for Dick Carroll, editor of the newly-formed Gold Medal series at Fawcett publishing. Gold Medal had been deliberately created by Fawcett to specialize in original paperback fiction—that is, fiction that had not first been released in hardcover and then released in paperback—and Meaker provided the publisher with its first lesbian pulp. In 1952 under the name of Vin Packer, Meaker wrote *Spring Fire*, which had an immediate impact. It was the first original lesbian pulp produced in the United States (Dick Carroll had been inspired to print a lesbian pulp because of the success of French author Tereska Torres's 1950 *Women's Barracks*, reprinted by the Feminist Press in 2005). Like most pulps, it was designed for a specific market, and like most pulps, it exceeded that market. The pulps' titillating covers, lurid blurbs, and back cover copy, their cheap paper and low price, and their size made them, as their publishers had hoped, the choice of commuters and casual readers alike.

What we now call lesbian pulps comprised a loose collection of fiction that featured lesbian themes and characters, no matter how unimportant or tangential to the plot. Such fiction was purchased by men, but it found its way also into the hands of lesbian readers. Since publishing houses often had strict editorial guidelines for content, sometimes guided by the fear of having books impounded, sometimes guided by the success of a previous book, most lesbian pulps, whether written by women or men, ended with a heterosexual union of some kind, even if, as in the work of Valerie Taylor and Ann

Bannon, the lesbian characters and lesbian experience were represented as neither dangerous, nor emotionally immature, nor pathological. Even though Vin Packer's *Spring Fire* ended as so many other lesbian pulps that followed it ended, this novel found an audience of lesbians. Ann Bannon, the most famous and most reprinted lesbian pulp novelist, loved *Spring Fire* so much that she wrote a fan letter to Vin Packer, who then brokered the meeting between Bannon and Carroll which resulted in the famous Beebo Brinker series of Gold Medal pulps.

Paperback Revolution and Sexuality

Much scholarship on pulps and pulp presses in lesbian literary and cultural histories has focused on novels (Stryker 2001, Zimet 1999). Gay and straight scholars alike have looked at how the pulps brokered the appearance of social minorities as subjects and as writers of novels. Many have also looked carefully at how the relatively formulaic narrative conventions of the pulps shaped how lesbians could establish themselves as authors and as writers (Foote 2005, Keller 2005, Walters 1989, Villarejo 1999). The history and politics of what has become known as the "paperbacking revolution" are as relevant for understanding the shape of Ann Aldrich's career as they are for understanding Marijane Meaker's career. Paperback originals established Meaker as a professional writer— Vin Packer, who had a long, well-regarded career, wrote mysteries that were reviewed in the prestigious *New York Times Book Review*, for example—and their particular textual and artifactual qualities (the way they looked, their covers, their size, their price) are all relevant to understanding how and in what company Ann Aldrich's books would have first appeared to readers. The work of pulp novels is important for reconstructing a range of lesbian cultures, but it is also important to understand the forces that produced and limited a larger paperbacking revolution that produced presses like Gold Medal. Those presses did not simply broker the emergence of new kinds of fiction. They produced new relationships between authors and readers, and in turn they provided a place for readers to encounter people who had until very recently been considered deviants, criminals, or medical "cases."

What we now think of as the golden age of pulp fiction, especially the golden age of gay and lesbian pulp fiction, with its interest in dangerous sexual alliances and its assimilation of new readers and writers, was not a small, somewhat disreputable segment of the book trade. *Publishers Weekly*, the standard trade journal for publishers and booksellers, inaugurated a section called "The Mass Market" in 1953, estimating that "paper books account for about 35 per cent of the whole dollar sales of books of all kinds" ("The Mass Market" 1953, 2101). Paperbacks could travel to outlets that didn't stock hardcover books, and a given press could produce a range of different kinds of paperbacks. Anchor and Gold Medal and Crown published a range of fiction and nonfiction, and in the process they blurred the line between high and low, information and titillation. The pulp publisher Pocket Books, for example, reprinted respected titles from its hardcover parent, McGraw Hill, on cheap paper, with the requisite lurid blurbs on the cover. John Knight's *The Story of My Psychoanalysis* is a good example. First printed in 1950 in hardback, it was reissued in paperback in 1952. The book looks cheap and lurid, but the text is a surprisingly thoughtful first-person account describing one man's psychoanalysis and embodying the popularization of Freudian theories of the self. More practically the list of paperbacks dealing with sexuality branched out into nonfiction, or at least, were marketed as nonfiction, in order to evade postal regulations; novels might be considered obscene but "scientific books," for which the Kinsey report had created a market, were far less stringently policed than novels. The paperbacking industry was something of a bell-wether for obscenity cases. Obscenity laws and community movements were different in various locations, and paperback publishers sometimes deliberately challenged obscenity laws by testing what could be shipped or sold in various geographic locations in the United States ("Pocket Books to Test Michigan Obscenity Laws" 1954).[1] The overlap between lurid pulps and serious pulps and the possibility of a book being judged obscene and therefore being repressed and made invisible, created a space for the production and the reception of Ann Aldrich's work. Aldrich's books fit neatly into no established genre, but they were part of a general interest in sexuality that itself was indebted, as Ann Aldrich writes in *We Walk Alone*, to "a climate of concern with all things psychological" (154).

The range of texts in the fifties and sixties dealing with sexuality of any sort was astonishing. The idiom of a popular sexuality and a popular Freudian self-analysis was available for consumption not only in pulps, but in a range of books that straddled the border between official documents meant to be read only by medical experts and popular books available to anyone. Publishers like Cadillac were dedicated to printing advice manuals, marriage manuals, specializing in sex advice manuals such as *The Illustrated Encyclopedia of Sex*, which promised "lasting mutual satisfaction for all couples" (*Sexology* 1952, back cover). A number of sociological texts about lesbianism were produced by the same pulp publishers who specialized in lurid tales of deviant love; indeed, it was often difficult to tell the difference between genuine and faintly pornographic "studies" of lesbians. For example, Hasselrodt's *Lesbianism Around the World* (1963) is a collection of factoids about lesbian relationships in numerous countries, and it is copiously footnoted. Hanson's *Secret Lesbian Society* (1965), on the other hand, is soft porn held together by the story of an undercover female news reporter. All of these texts rely on a fairly popularized psychoanalytic idiom and many of them can cite—some glibly, some more seriously—legal precedents and Kinsey-like sexological data. Most rely on "personal" anecdotes, which reference a fully elaborated culture of gays and lesbians that existed just below the radar in large urban areas.

All these texts struggle with the definition of gay sexuality. Within various books—popular scientific, clinical sexuality, psychoanalysis, fiction—lines of tension over exactly how people became gay crossed and recrossed. Some writers relied on the theory that gays and lesbians were hardwired as "deviants" and should therefore be tolerated in society and under the law. Others espoused a theory that gay and lesbian people were socially produced, either through trauma or circumstances (prisons and boarding schools figure in such accounts) or through distorted family dynamics to which popular Freudianism was often reduced.

What suddenly made it possible for sexuality to be critical in a range of texts, and what made it possible for the topic to be discussed in many idioms as well as repressed by many local censors? Clearly, Kinsey was a factor. By 1953, just before Ann Aldrich's first book came out, Kinsey had released his *Sexual Behavior in the Human Female* (*Sexual Behavior in the Human Male* had appeared in 1948). Among the most controversial of his arguments was that an extraordinary number of men and women had had homosexual relations at some point in their lives. Both books also introduced social analysis to the study of sexuality. Kinsey correlated such factors as age, class, and educational level with sexual experiences, without arguing that such factors caused particular kinds of sexuality. The effect of Kinsey's book was immediate. *Publishers Weekly*'s anonymous "Note on *About the Kinsey Report*" reported in 1948 that interest in Kinsey's work was so high that a book that merely interpreted Kinsey's findings had actually outsold the Kinsey report

(2629). Five years later, *Publishers Weekly* announced the release of a medical book that aimed to counter aggressively the Kinsey's view of female sexuality ("Note on *Response to the Kinsey Report*" 1953, 2467).

In some places, Kinsey's work enabled the circulation of new knowledge. For example, *Sexology*, the journal dedicated to popularizing information about sexuality and sexual pleasure, routinely included articles on lesbianism, its causes and cures, as well as letters from readers who sought information about homosexuality. In January 1952 Mr. R.R. of California wrote, "In recent years I have been physically attracted to certain men." Combined with his enjoyment of silk underwear, he had begun to suspect that he was either a homosexual or a fetishist or both. The editors concluded, following a relatively long response, "assuredly you have homosexual tendencies" (R.R. 1952, 391). In the same issue, however, the editors wrote lengthily to a man interested in lesbianism and "sexual deviations," telling him about books on the subject published by the New Book Company, the very organization that had purchased advertising in its pages. *Sexology* included at least one letter in every issue in the 1950s from readers who suspected that they were homosexuals, and after the Kinsey report was released, the editors consulted Dr. Kinsey for many of its articles. In every issue this magazine included information about books on homosexuality, including publishers' addresses.

Even in the most conventionally respectable publications, moreover, sexuality—its meaning, its origin, its function in the creation of families, communities, and nations—was a major topic, further underscoring that in the 1950s sexuality was debated in strikingly similar terms in very different venues directed at very different audiences. For example, around the same time that Marijane Meaker was writing the first few of her five books in the Ann Aldrich series, *Time* magazine ran a

series of articles and notes about homosexuality, both in the
United States and Britain. Much of their coverage reviewed
official reports or analyses of homosexuality and its causes, and
although the coverage often included ominous warnings that
homosexuals tended to form a monolithic society that could
threaten mainstream society, the main goal seemed focused on
the possibility of improving the lives of individual homosexuals. In a positive review of Edmund Bergler's 1956 *Homosexuality: Disease or Way of Life? Time* wrote approvingly that
Bergler's book corrected "some recent misleading propaganda
alleg[ing] that homosexuality is an incurable hereditary condition, and that the homosexual way of life is therefore 'normal'
for an unspecified proportion of the population." *Time* also
carried coverage of "The Wolfenden Report," the 1957 British
government's report that in part recommended that homosexuality be decriminalized. *The Nation*, a more liberal periodical
than *Time*, allowed itself more than *Time*'s thinly veiled disap-
proval in its discussions of the topic. In "The Homosexual
Challenge to Science," a long survey of current work on sexuality, the author, George Silver, assumed that the reader wished
to understand contemporary debates, and provided an
overview of anthropological, sexological, and psychological literature on the topic (1957).

Lesbian Publishing in the Fifties

Finally, although the popular press enabled it, Aldrich's work is
connected to another print venue and another sexual culture.
Her first book was released at the same time as the first nation-
ally conceived gay and lesbian publications and organizations.
In 1955, the very year that *We Walk Alone* was published, the
Daughters of Bilitis (DOB)—the first national association of
lesbians—was formed, and in 1956, the first issue of its magazine, *The Ladder*, appeared. The magazine *ONE*, founded by
ONE, Inc (which had developed out of the larger *Mattachine*

Society) had begun to print (in 1953), and in 1955 the *Mattachine Society* began the monthly *Mattachine Review*. In 1956 Jeanette Foster published her important reference work *The Sex Variant Woman in Literature*.

The Ladder in particular is an important historical contemporary of Aldrich's work. Although Aldrich was writing about lesbian cultures in New York, and the DOB and *The Ladder* were based in California, each took seriously the task of addressing the testimony of experts on the subject of women's sexuality. *The Ladder*'s editors engaged often and directly with members of the medical and psychiatric community, inviting debate from its members on various theories as well as searching out members of that community who did not pathologize lesbianism (indeed, conversing with that community was part of the mission statement of *The Ladder*). As important, the editors of *The Ladder* recognized that the ability of lesbians to organize—even if only in print—could combat the intense scrutiny of a putatively deviant individual. A single person is a patient; a group of people form a community. Despite the DOB's reputation for seeking to assimilate into mainstream culture—a reading that dismisses the disputatious tone of the journal's editorials, journalism, and letters during the fifties— its leaders were also interested in the consequences of assimilation into an inhospitable mainstream culture.

If we see Ann Aldrich's work intersecting with popular fiction, semi-popular and quasi-scientific texts about sexuality, and newly emerging gay and lesbian publications, we must also recognize that it situated itself in response to yet another expert on gay sexuality. In 1951, Donald Webster Cory published his study *The Homosexual in America* (1957). In his preface, Cory writes: "This book is the result of a quarter of a century of participation in American life as a homosexual. I am convinced that there is a need for dissemination of information and for a free exchange of argument and opinion on this subject. It is my belief that the observations and viewpoints of the homosexual are as essential as those of the psychiatrist, the jurist, or the churchman in arriving at any conclusions on homosexuality" (xiii). Cory argues that despite the fact that he is relying on his own experiences as a gay man that "the majority of homosexuals will be able to identify themselves with the thoughts and experiences related in many sections of this work" (xiii). Widely read and reviewed, Cory's study provoked debate among critics. *The Nation*, in a guarded and ambivalent review, argued that it is so committed to the idea that homosexuality could not be cured that it "ends up almost as a promotional job" (Sapirstein 1951, 552). By deliberately citing the opening sentences of *The Homosexual in America*, and transforming them into her own opening sentences, Aldrich's text acknowledges that gay people are experts about their own experiences and lives, and also points out the relative invisibility of lesbians in discussions of gay life—even discussions by gay men.

We Walk Alone echoes Donald Webster Cory in its organization as well: Aldrich includes information about literary history, classical and European history, contemporary legal and medical views of homosexuality, as well as an extremely informative discussion regarding state laws' definitions of homosexual behavior and the punishments thereof. In all this, she addresses the realities of lesbians, who were relatively invisible in magazine and medical accounts of homosexuality.

The Narrative Voice

Beyond the historical contexts of Ann Aldrich's work, readers may still be surprised by the contents of *We Walk Alone*, for the text combines anecdotes, gossip, a tour of bars, historical evaluations, challenges to the medical profession, and sometimes extraordinarily intimate moments of self-analysis. Yet uniting all is Aldrich's wonderfully compelling narrative voice. Assured, wry, world-weary, and acutely observant, Aldrich's tone is sometimes as measured and careful as a sociologist's, and sometimes as impassioned as a political organizer's. She is sometimes regally dismissive of professional verdicts and definitions of homosexuality, sometimes slyly in accord with them (often against their intentions), and she is sometimes even surprisingly contemptuous and judgmental about some lesbians within her anecdotes. She can sum up a topic in a biting bon mot, and the next moment be as briskly comforting as an advice columnist. The compelling quality of *We Walk Alone* hangs on Aldrich's voice, its subtle modulations, its self-possession. The text is written by a crack novelist/journalist who knows how to tell a story, or rather a series of stories.

How do lesbians read the world that reads them? How does Aldrich read that dynamic? The narrative energy of *We Walk Alone* emerges from Aldrich's stance as a participant and observer. Movement between these two positions disrupts any single narrative that can account for or define "the lesbian." Take, for example, her first chapter, "Who Is She?" A young man confides to the narrator of *We Walk Alone* that he can always spot a lesbian. He reels off a list of stereotypes that look uncomfortably similar to those that still exist:

> [Lesbians] are good at sports; indeed . . . most gym teachers are "lessies," as are a majority of women athletes. Lesbians drink more than most women, and they drink their liquor "neat" or "on the rocks." Lesbians want careers; they like to "show men up" in the business world. Lesbians are more intellectual than average females; they read more, know more about art and music and scoff at men who aren't interested in these things. (2)

It is not difficult to discern that many of the common stereotypes that the confident young man shares with Ann Aldrich describe all ambitious and successful women. Indeed, it's rather clear that lesbianism pathologizes for him all female deviance, including professional ambition. But Aldrich includes this laundry list of popular misconceptions, of which I have quoted only a few, so that she can say with dramatic flourish:

> Who is the lesbian?
>   She is many women.
>   Look at her, and she cannot be distinguished from her more normal sisters. . . . There is no stereotype in the over-all picture of the lesbian. This is the first discovery I ever made about the group of which I am a member. (3)

Later in the same chapter, she writes definitively: "I have seen them often, known them, watched them, listened to them, talked with them, lived with them, and been a part of their life. I have seen them, and I am one of them; yet I have never been able to pick a lesbian out of a crowd. There is no definition, no formula, no pattern that will accurately characterize the female homosexual" (6).

Structurally the chapter establishes a pattern that recurs throughout the book: Aldrich begins with an anecdote related to her, in this first instance by a young man who seems to embody the popular educated view of lesbianism. After she elaborates this anecdote, she refutes it as well as the popular wisdom of which it forms a part, advancing a more capacious analysis in its place. She addresses the work of professional researchers of homosexuality, and then measures their findings against her own observations as an insider. Those observations are deeply detailed, each organized as a vignette about some aspect of lesbian life. In this case, her own observations—about crushes in boarding schools, butch bars, upscale parties, sororities—gain momentum and gravitas though her use of anaphoric sentences to underline her experiential authority. "I have seen," she writes, again and again. Substantively, the chapter establishes the ground on which Aldrich can rest her fundamental insight that lesbians do not form one, but many cultures, and that those cultures are, as Raymond Williams wrote at around the same time Aldrich was writing, whole ways of life (1989).

As soon as she makes room for any woman as a lesbian, Aldrich takes the reader on both a historical and a geographic tour, a strategy that had worked for Donald Webster Cory. A good deal of the early lesbian literature she cites, moreover, particularly the high modernist work of Djuna Barnes or Natalie Barney, was already well known. Combined with historical information on ancient Greek civilizations, Aldrich could suggest that lesbianism was neither a modern pathology, nor an aberrance that strikes only a few unlucky or confused women. Indeed, claiming lesbian artists and writers was a time-honored tradition for claiming that same-sex love, or a form of emotional intimacy outside of conventional heterodoxy, could impart creativity and analytical ability. Literary women evoke a past to be shared both with a general population and with one another.

Aldrich yokes history to space, for same-sex love has carved out spaces and created networks across geographic boundaries. She organizes her book around particular people in very specific places—"the Marks of Greenwich Village, the Vances of Paris, and the Kittys of Sutton Place" (77). In these spaces people gather of different social classes, backgrounds, dispositions, ages, regions, and nationalities. Whether a swank apartment or a dank bar, each space contains what Aldrich thinks of as a different instance of lesbian culture—in which factors other than sexual preference might be the most important criteria for membership. "The only way to know the lesbian," she writes, "is to meet the many women she is at close range; to see her against her various backgrounds" (42). The boundaries between lesbian cultures are permeable, of course. Women can move between them. On matters of race the text is relatively silent, speaking perhaps to a more entrenched division in culture at large, one that ironically found it easier to talk about sexual deviance than racial difference. In the case of "butches," class issues are intensified because such lesbians must either pass as men (and live in fear of discovery) or they must find a job in queer spaces. It is, however, gender's relationship to class (among white women) that catches Ann Aldrich's eye; her sensitivity toward gender issues as they are imbricated in class issues is one of the heretofore unappreciated gifts of the book.

For Aldrich, social divisions around gender are structuring elements of the socially constructed geography of the city. The spaces that lesbians carved out in the fifties enabled them to find lovers and friends, to gather as new family in homelike neighborhoods and bars. And yet the spatial segregation that was understood to exist between various groups of lesbians was also in some sense disabling, especially for working-class women. They were at the mercy of police, who could raid a bar and arrest its inhabitants, and of bar owners who could overcharge them (even if only to cover the cost of paying off the police). Aldrich is as sharp as any investigative reporter as she looks carefully at how material issues—jobs, money, clothes, physical space—affect women as a class as well as women in particular classes.

The Cultural Historian

Of course, this makes some of Aldrich's depictions of many of the lesbians she describes appear to be that much more biting, and in some sense, that much more inexplicable. So clearly aware of the ways in which lesbian culture and straight culture alike shaped the range of choices available for women, and so sensitive to the ways in which the innumerable factors that make up any culture change both its members and are changed by them, why does Ann Aldrich seem, at points, to dismiss or degrade some of the people she discusses? Sensitive to class issues, she will still revile the "butch." She will write that a little girl who notices that "outdoor plumbing" on boys differentiates the genders will also inevitably notice that there are "social privileges connected with being a man" (21), underscoring the "disadvantages" (21) of being a woman in a male-dominated world. But she will also say that it is fear that makes a lesbian, "fear of the 'snips and snails of puppy dogs' tails.' Fear of pregnancy. Fear of submission, penetration, and the possibility of ensuing rejection" (24). This fear will change a "normal girl into a homosexual woman" (24). Here she has moved from a social critique to a psychological diagnosis, not pausing to connect the two.

To take another example, how can Aldrich write "gay life for the female homosexual, as lived in the gay bars and cafes of the world, is a lonely, harassed and depressing life" (67), or "whether she is a perpetual tomboy who has yet to don high heels, a silk dress, and lipstick to brave the world of grownups, or whether she is a charming and very feminine 'adult child,' [the lesbian] is an immature and abnormal woman" (24)? As she seems to agree with both Sappho and Freud, de Beauvoir and Ellis, she swings back and forth between impatience with what she seems to understand as a self-victimization on the one hand, and scorn for the attempt to find one single explanation for lesbianism on the other. Aldrich's practicality, that is, often seems at odds with her scholar's mind. At exactly the moment she seems to come down on the side of nascent social constructionism (fear of pregnancy is a powerful social factor for women in the fifties, not merely an instance of fear of men in general), she considers a classically dismissive psychological explanation, like narcissism. At exactly the moment she critiques lesbian cultures that she finds in bars and neighborhoods, she reflects on the social ostracism that can destroy a woman who is outed. Sometimes Aldrich herself seems to make women into psychological case studies, and sometimes she seems indifferent to the analytic utility of "cases."

Aldrich is contradictory, and there is no way to reconcile some of those contradictions. In fact, once we accept that Ann Aldrich is something of an agent provocateur, it is easier, rather than more difficult to see the value in what she is doing. One of Ann Aldrich's missions in this book was to show that no one could tell who was or would be a lesbian, a desire in some sense to critique what we might call a social as well as a psychological method of diagnosing all women and their sexuality. In order to do this, she schooled herself in some of the regnant psychological theories of the fifties, and again, it is a tribute to her work, and a debt that we owe her, that she did not simply reject or dismiss psychiatry, nor simply embrace it and celebrate it. Rather, she tried, just as she did with the lesbian cultures she approached, to understand the social life of psychology, its uses, its desires, and its different cultures. She did not flatten out medical practitioners; rather she responded to them. Her experience was her expertise, and she used it efficiently, combining it with attention to the expertise that the psychiatric community had developed.

As a cultural historian of perversion, and a perverse one at that, Ann Aldrich told people something before they could really hear it: Every historical moment yields multiple choices and possibilities, and multiple futures repose together in the past. If the mainstream press believed that queer culture would form its own society, Ann Aldrich believed that this could not, and should not happen, for it would force homosexuals to conform to it in precisely the ways that they had to conform to a heterosexual world. This is what Ann Aldrich was so insightful in recognizing: Lesbians didn't have a preordained destiny and would not experience or live their lesbianism in the same way. Always attentive to the differences people could make historically, Aldrich's sometimes cruel jabs weren't merely aimed at individuals, but at an emerging orthodoxy that might (as she strategically did herself) produce stereotypes in contradiction to the fullness with which she tried to present their world.

Responses: Then and Now

As with any text, once *We Walk Alone* left the hands of its author and went into the world, it became the subject of interpretation by readers Aldrich could not have anticipated. In her Foreword she writes:

> It is my wish that *We Walk Alone* may bring more compassionate understanding on the part of mothers and fathers, sisters and brothers, friends, teachers, employers and strangers, who may at some time in their lives be confronted with homosexuality in their midst. I hope too that my book will contribute something toward encouraging a greater tolerance of this minority, and that it will hearten those homosexuals, like myself, who are earnestly trying to resolve the perplexing problems that face them in their daily living (xii).

Although it appears that the book is addressed to virtually everyone, Aldrich, knowing as well as she did the differences in lesbian cultures, could not have expected that every lesbian would read the book, nor that every lesbian culture described within it would approve or even agree with her project. Indeed, the response to *We Walk Alone* might be one of its most interesting elements. As scholars reclaim this text, and are drawn to those who followed it, it's important to keep in mind not only the world that produced the book, but the world that it in turn helped to produce.

The book has elicited rather strong responses since it was published, and in very material ways, those responses are now part of the text of the rest of Aldrich's work. Aldrich paid attention to them, and quite literally incorporated them into her next book. *We Walk Alone* was popular; it was reprinted several times, and from the beginning, it elicited letters from readers all over the United States. Some wanted more explicit information about where to find lesbians in New York; others wanted to criticize Aldrich's findings; still others wanted affirmation and a conversation with another lesbian. They wanted to know that they were not alone. For many readers, New York was a golden land, a place where they could find a community of lesbians ready to welcome them; *We Walk Alone* was a signpost leading to this golden country. While it was widely read in New York, it was also widely read outside of New York. Clearly, the book affected a diverse group of people; Ann Aldrich reached a larger and perhaps a slightly different audience than the one she had anticipated. A few of the letters that she received were reprinted in her next book, *We, Too, Must Love* (1958), in part a response to those letters, a text constructed in relationship not to an abstract or ideal audience, but directed to an audience which had tried to announce itself to her.

We, Too, Must Love, like its predecessor, was written at the moment of an emerging popular cultural concern with sexuality, and like its predecessor it was written within an increasingly vocal world of gay and lesbian print—one that Ann Aldrich had helped to create. *We Walk Alone* had brought all sorts of people into its ambit, and into a wide community of diverse readers. This is especially worth remembering as we try to account for later responses to this text.

The Daughters of Bilitis passionately disliked Ann

Aldrich, although their response to her was more tempered in the beginning. They held a roundtable on the book, and concluded that the book had many shortcomings, some of which could be chalked up to the exigencies of "commercial publishing" ("Aldrich 'Walks Alone'" 1957, 16).[2] But the roundtable also "generally agreed that Miss Aldrich 'tried,' that hers is a valid contribution to Lesbian literature (of which there is so little) if not taken too seriously" (17). As the fifties faded out, and gay and lesbian politics became more militant, Ann Aldrich's work was considered "self-hating," a dangerous, if not shameful relic of a dark time in gay history. For example, although they mimic much of Aldrich's debunking of lesbian stereotypes, Del Martin and Phyllis Lyon wrote that Aldrich dwelt "mostly on bizarre examples" (1972, 22), and Barbara Grier wrote that having Ann Aldrich "publishing actively is much like having a snake in one's bedclothing" (1976, 39). These opinions tell us less about *We Walk Alone* than they do about the process of consolidating a politics that, in the name of including more lesbians, and being more vocal and proud of diversity in the lesbian community, needed to officially misread one of the books that first described the potential diversity of the lesbian world.

We Walk Alone was an influential book, and it has sparked major debate. As the gay and lesbian community began to organize in the sixties and seventies, seeking a more radical political platform and beginning to rethink the idea of identity and its relationship to sexuality, Ann Aldrich first received severe criticism, and then was forgotten. The complexity and cosmopolitan cynicism of the book's tone was flattened out, perceived as merely scornful or derisive, and her insistence that lesbianism could not be understood outside of local contexts was lost. The irony is, of course, that Aldrich was perceived as being dated, blind to the worst problems of the fifties, despite the fact that her goal had been to interrogate the tendency of her historical moment to flatten out sexual identities, to assign single and uncomplicated meanings to them. We are finally ready to hear what Ann Aldrich had to say in her earliest work. Far from being an example of a pre–Stonewall false consciousness, Ann Aldrich is an important forerunner for gay and lesbian culture, for she understood, perhaps long before her audience was ready to hear from her, that no single definition could encompass the identities, choices, and desires of lesbians.

Stephanie Foote
Urbana, Illinois
June 2006

Notes

1. Although Kinsey was clearly among the exempted scientific writers, his attempt to create an archive of sexological photos, paintings, statues, books, and magazines by importing them from all over the world subjected him to censorship under obscenity laws ("Kinsey's Imports Seized; Sees Threat to Scholars' Rights" 1956). The obscenity laws were both very strict and very loose in the fifties. In 1953 under the House of Representatives Select Committee on Current Pornographic Materials, or the Gathings Committee, the Post Office was empowered to decide on what was obscene. At the same time the definition of obscenity was changing, and many obscenity cases were local. *Publishers Weekly* kept a close eye on all obscenity cases. It covered the Gathings Committee Reports, as well as local instances of book banning ("Gathings Committee Reports on 'Pornographic' Books" 1953). One editorial remarked, "The general picture of censorship reveals a pattern which is of concern to the entire book trade—the pattern of rapidly increasing local pressures and . . . the wholesale condemnation of books, *not judged by due process* and by competent authorities but by many amateur self-appointed censors" ("Book Censorship Is Reaching Epidemic Proportions" 1953, 1060, emphasis in original).

2. For accounts of the relationship between Ann Aldrich and the Daughters of Bilitis see "Aldrich 'Walks Alone'" 1957, Meeker 2005b, and my afterword to Ann Aldrich's *We, Too, Must Love*.

Works Cited

Aldrich, Ann. 1955. *We Walk Alone*. Greenwich, CT: Fawcett/Gold Medal.

———. 1958. *We, Too, Must Love*. Greenwich, CT: Fawcett/Gold Medal.

———. 1960. *Carol in a Thousand Cities*. Greenwich, CT: Fawcett/Gold Medal.

———. 1963. *We Two Won't Last*. Greenwich, CT: Fawcett/Gold Medal.

———. 1972. *Take a Lesbian to Lunch*. New York: McFadden.

"Aldrich 'Walks Alone.'" 1957. *The Ladder* 1:9 (June): 16–17.

Bergler, Edmund. 1956. *Homosexuality: Disease or Way of Life?* New York: Hill and Wang.

"Book Censorship Is Reaching Epidemic Proportions." 1953. *Publishers Weekly* 163:59

(February 28):1058–1060.

Cory, Donald Webster. 1957. *The Homosexual in America: A Subjective Approach*. [1951]. New York: Greenberg Publishers.

"Curable Disease?" 1956. *Time Magazine* Dec. 10:74, 76.

Duberman, Martin, Martha Vicinus, and George Chauncey. 1990. *Hidden from History: Reclaiming the Gay and Lesbian Past*. [1989]. New York: Plume Books.

Foote, Stephanie. 2005. "Deviant Classics: Pulps and the Making of Lesbian Print Culture." *Signs* 31:1 (Autumn):169–189.

Foster, Jeannette H. 1985. *Sex Variant Women in Literature*. [1956]. Tallahassee, FL. Naiad Press.

"Gathings Committee Reports on 'Pornographic' Books." 1953. *Publishers Weekly* 163:2 (January 10):125–127.

Grier, Barbara. 1976. *Lesbiana: Book Reviews from The Ladder 1966–1972*. Tallahassee, FL. Naiad Press.

Hale, Arthur. 1953. "The Mass Market." *Publishers Weekly* 164:21 (Nov 21):2101.

Hanson, Doris. 1965. *Secret Lesbian Society*. New York: Imperial Books of L.S. Publications.

Hasselrodt, R. Leighton. 1963. *Lesbianism Around the World*. New York: A Midwood Book of Tower Publications.

Keller, Yvonne. 2005. "'Was it Right to Love Her Brother's Wife So Passionately?' Lesbian Pulp Novels and US Lesbian Identity, 1950–1965." *American Quarterly*. 57:1 (June):385–410.

Kinsey, Alfred C. 1953. *Sexual Behavior in the Human Female*. Philadelphia: Saunders.

"Kinsey's Imports Seized; Sees Threat to Scholars' Rights." 1956. *Publishers Weekly* 170:8 (August 20):786.

Knight, John. 1952. *The Story of My Psychoanalysis*. [1950]. New York: Pocket Books.

Macherey, Pierre. 1992. *A Theory of Literary Production*. [1978]. New York: Routledge.

Martin, Del and Phyllis Lyon. 1972. *Lesbian/Woman*. San Francisco: Glide Publications.

Meaker, Marijane. 2003. *Highsmith: A Romance of the Fifties*. San Francisco: Cleis Press.

Meeker, Martin. 2005a. "Pulp Legacy: An Interview with Marijane Meaker." *Lambda Book Report* 13 (Jan–March):6–8.

———. 2005b. "A Queer and Contested Medium: The Emergence of Representational Politics in the 'Golden Age' of Lesbian Paperbacks, 1955–1963." *Journal of Women's History* 17:1 (Spring):165–188.

"Note on *About the Kinsey Report*." 1948. *Publishers Weekly* 153:26 (June 26):2629.

"Note on *Response to the Kinsey Report*." 1953. *Publishers Weekly* 164:26 (December 26):2467.

Packer, Vin. 2004. *Spring Fire*. [1952]. San Francisco: Cleis Press, 2004.

"Pocket Books to Test Michigan Obscenity Laws." 1954. *Publishers Weekly* 166:4 (July 24):365–6.

R.R., Mr. 1952. Letter. *Sexology* (January):391.

Sapirstein, Milton R. 1951. "The 'Happy' Homosexual." *The Nation* Dec 22:551–552.

Silver, George. 1957. "The Homosexual Challenge to Science." *The Nation* May 25:451–454. *Sexology: Sex Science Magazine*. 1952. Advertisement for Cadillac Press's *The Illustrated Encyclopedia of Sex*. (January) 18:6.

Stryker, Susan. 2001. *Queer Pulp: Perverted Passions from the Golden Age of the Paperback*. San Francisco: Chronicle Press.

Torres, Tereska. 2005. *Women's Barracks*. [1950]. New York: The Feminist Press.

Villarejo, Amy. 1999. "Forbidden Love: Pulp as Lesbian History." In *Out Takes: Essays on Queer Theory and Film*, edited by Ellis Hanson. Durham, NC: Duke University Press.

Walters, Suzanna Danuta. 1989. "As Her Hand Crept Slowly Up Her Thigh: Ann Bannon and the Politics of Pulp." *Social Text* 23 (Fall–Winter):83–101.

Williams, Raymond. 1989. "Culture is Ordinary" in *Resources of Hope*. London: Verso.

"The Wolfenden Report." 1957. *Time Magazine* Sept 16:39–40.

Zimet, Jaye. 1999. *The Art of Lesbian Pulp Fiction, 1949-1969*. New York: Viking Studio Books.